DEVIL'S ADVOCATES

DEVIL'S ADVOCATES is a series of books devoted to exploring the classics of horror cinema. Contributors to the series come from the fields of teaching, academia, journalism and fiction, but all have one thing in common: a passion for the horror film and a desire to share it with the widest possible audience.

'The admirable Devil's Advocates series is not only essential – and fun – reading for the serious horror fan but should be set texts on any genre course.'
Dr Ian Hunter, Reader in Film Studies, De Montfort University, Leicester

'Auteur Publishing's new Devil's Advocates critiques on individual titles... offer bracingly fresh perspectives from passionate writers. The series will perfectly complement the BFI archive volumes.' **Christopher Fowler,** *Independent on Sunday*

'Devil's Advocates has proven itself more than capable of producing impassioned, intelligent analyses of genre cinema... quickly becoming the go-to guys for intelligent, easily digestible film criticism.' *Horror Talk.com*

'Auteur Publishing continue the good work of giving serious critical attention to significant horror films.' *Black Static*

 DevilsAdvocatesbooks

DevilsAdBooks

DEVIL'S ADVOCATES

DAWN OF THE DEAD

JON TOWLSON

auteur

Acknowledgements

My thanks to the following people for making this project possible: John Atkinson at Auteur/LUP; Richard Cooper at *Scream*; Chris Holden at Second Sight Films; Adam Charles Hart and Benjamin T. Rubin at the George A. Romero Archive, University of Pittsburgh; Jacob Smith at the British Board of Film Classification; Sam Wigley at the British Film Institute.

I am grateful to the following for their help and support: Paul R. Gagne, James Gracey, Joseph Maddrey, Kendall R. Phillips, Jeff Wolfe and, as always, my wife (and fellow zombie movie fan), Joanne Rudling.

Thanks also to staffs at the JB Morrell Library, University of York and the Brotherton Library, University of Leeds for their help in accessing research materials.

First published in 2022 by
Auteur, an imprint of
Liverpool University Press,
4 Cambridge Street,
Liverpool
L69 7ZU

Series design: Nikki Hamlett at Cassels Design
Set by Cassels Design, Luton UK
Printed and bound by CPI Group (UK) Ltd, Croydon CR0 4YY

British Library Cataloguing-in-Publication Data
A catalogue record for this book is available from the British Library

ISBN paperback: 978-1-80085-638-7
ISBN hardback: 978-1-80085-637-0
ISBN PDF: 978-1-80085-515-1

CONTENTS

Publicity still for Dawn of the Dead *(1978) (l to r): Roger (Scott H. Reiniger), Fran (Gaylen Ross), Stephen (David Emge) and Peter (Ken Foree) seize the shopping mall from rampaging zombies.*

INTRODUCTION: "SUPERSCHLOCK"

After the 1979 Dallas Film Festival screening of *Dawn of the Dead* at the Bob Hope Theater on Southern Methodist University Campus, George A. Romero was accosted by a group of outraged silver-haired women in their diamonds and jewels. These Junior Leaguers had walked out of *Dawn*'s first US public showing less than 15 minutes into the movie, and had been lying in wait for the director outside the picture house. "You're not fooling us!" they protested. "That film was just a schlock movie disguised as art!" To their surprise, Romero appeared to agree with them. "There's no disguise involved," he demurred. "It's just schlock. In fact, it's superschlock."[1]

George A. Romero long contended that *Dawn of the Dead* was nothing more than schlock, a combination of (as he told *Starburst* in 1982) "all the schlock classics that we have had over the past 20 or 30 years".[2] For him, the social satire that critics praise *Dawn* for was always part of the surface excess, "very frontal, very obvious… it is criticism from overstatement. It's overkill and obviously so. It carries things to an absurd degree that we know is absurd."[3] Perhaps it was that very excess that divided the Dallas audience, twenty per cent of whom left in disgust (with those who remained violently hissing those who were leaving). In his on-stage interview with Roger Ebert following the screening, Romero remarked: "You can say the movie is an observation about materialism, and so forth, and what have you really said? The point is that people come out of the film having experienced some very extreme emotions, and it's up to them to interpret what happened."[4]

Arguably, excess is at the heart of *Dawn of the Dead*, integral to its meaning, not only in its scenes of gore, its (custard pie) in-your-face social satire and its bawdy pop-kitsch style, but in the production history of the film itself. Romero took *Dawn* into new areas of extremity and in the process made perhaps the greatest horror film of the 1970s, a culmination of the American Nightmare cycle ("all the schlock classics") that began in 1968 with his own *Night of the Living Dead*.

One of the most perceptive comments made about *Dawn* is by a fan called The Red Duchess on IMDb who describes the film as a "reckless, hubristic, over-ambitious masterpiece whose excess is reined in by its Langian formal precision".[5] Romero's commitment to his craft was evident throughout his career, but the excess of *Dawn* had been equally deliberate. Romero started filming in November 1977 with a detailed screenplay that had, in his words, a "very pedantic kind of structure".[6] But when Romero edited the first half of *Dawn* together during a production shut down over the Christmas period, it seems he experienced a change of heart. Rather than wrap the movie and just use the footage that had been scripted, Romero and his cast and crew started to improvise whole new sections, adding more comedy, more action-adventure, more of an irreverent tone. Monroeville Mall's gaudy '70s pop atmosphere had only become truly apparent when photographed, and Romero clearly wanted to go with this new vibe to *Dawn* which seemed to him to speak of the times. And *Dawn*'s message was of the times. Every cultural and political commentator in the 1970s was bemoaning the consumer age, the effects of which had, according to social psychologist Erich Fromm, "created a climate of violence and destructiveness in the West".[7] Even the President of the United States, James Carter, was driven to admit (in a speech to the nation on July 15, 1979) that "too many of us now tend to worship self-indulgence and consumption. Human identity is no longer defined by what one does, but by what one owns. But we've discovered that owning things and consuming things does not satisfy our longing for meaning. We've learned that piling up material goods cannot fill the emptiness of lives which have no confidence or purpose."[8]

Dawn's excesses meant the film almost did not get distribution at all. Clocking in at well over two hours, when the average length of an exploitation movie back then was 90 minutes, *Dawn* was simply too long and too strong for the industry to take. The running time alone caused a number of distributors to back away. As Romero later complained in an interview with *Film Criticism*, "the industry can't handle a long running time… they want people in and out of the theatre in under two hours".[9] Consequently, *Dawn* challenged industry wisdom that horror films could not be epic.

In the US Romero held out not just for final cut but for the extreme gore scenes to stay intact. The threat of an "X"-rating made Warner Bros and American International Pictures walk. Eventually United Film Distribution Company (UFD), a subsidiary of the United Artists Theater Chain, agreed to distribute it uncut and unrated. *Dawn*'s resulting huge financial success pretty much ended the "X"-rating in America, as the *Pittsburgh Post-Gazette* observed in 1980: "When the ratings system started 10 years ago, most theaters refused to play unrated films, but this is no longer true. Anything that does business will be booked."[10] After *Dawn*, once-wary distributors were lining up to release their films unrated, with titles like *Bad Timing* (1980), *Zombie* (1979) and *Mother's Day* (1980) all being released without ratings.

Interestingly, it would be suburban audiences who would respond to *Dawn* the most. In its New York engagement it did better in New Rochelle than at the Rivoli on Broadway. Even in Pittsburgh, where *Dawn* made $55,000 in its first week, it took more at out of town theatres like Cinemette East and Cinema World than it did in Downtown Pittsburgh at the Gateway (where Romero was dismayed to walk in one Tuesday night to find fewer than 30 people in the audience). At the Cinemette East, audiences were lined up through the lobby. Across the parking lot, of course, was Monroeville Mall itself; even so, suburban audiences all over America seemed to understand *Dawn*, while city slicker critics like Vincent Canby, at *The New York Times*, derided Romero as the "Grandma Moses of exurban horror films".[11]

As Romero told *Starburst*, "*Dawn* is a celebration of schlock, not in a negative sense, and that was really all I was trying to say… I don't feel that in reflecting a negative human condition you in essence have to make a negative film."[12] Indeed, following movies like *The Last House on the Left* (1972) and *The Texas Chain Saw Massacre* (1974), *Dawn* marked a point of departure in the '70s apocalyptic horror cycle. It was, as film critic Robin Wood observed, "perhaps the first modern horror film to suggest – albeit very tentatively – the possibility of moving beyond apocalypse".[13] Before *Dawn*, contemporary horror movies seemed to end in total despair. *Dawn* was, by contrast, exhilarating in the way it gave audiences a glimmer of hope for humanity. Certainly, it remains one of the most optimistic horror films ever made.

Time has made *Dawn of the Dead* into a schlock classic, just like those of the past that inspired Romero. *Dawn* has now found almost universal critical approval as "one of the most compelling and entertaining zombie films ever" (*Rotten Tomatoes*);[14] but perhaps the greatest testament to *Dawn* is its fans, who still amass the Monroeville Mall today – *Dawn* conventions still take place there, and a fan-made bust of George A. Romero was recently unveiled alongside the mannequins and the mall-walkers.

With excess at the heart of *Dawn of the Dead*, this book explores the various ways in which Romero took *Dawn* into areas of extremity during its scripting, production and distribution, and the responses of industry, censorship bodies, reviewers and audiences of the time to the film's excesses. The approach I take is of a micro-historical study, a close analysis of the film's production context in order to explore the cultural significance of *Dawn of the Dead* as a 'rebel text'.

> [A]s a sort of anti-commodity, this underdog film's refusal to conform to norms of commodification did pay off... Credit is due, then, to the innovative and stubborn Romero whose apocalyptic vision of consumer society was successful in subverting consumer norms – A. Loudermilk, *Journal of Consumer Culture*, 2003.[15]

SCRIPTING A SATIRE OF CONSUMERISM

The idea for *Dawn* appears to have come from a friend of Romero who co-owned the Monroeville Mall, located fifteen miles outside of Pittsburgh. The development of huge out of town shopping malls across America in the 1970s was simultaneously a contributor to and symptom of the urban decline that led to downtown areas becoming no-go zones. As family businesses and small retailers closed as a result of mall development, inner city neighbourhoods became increasingly poverty-stricken. Romero had brilliantly essayed this kind of decay in his previous film, *Martin* (1977), set in the Pittsburgh suburb of Braddock.[16]

Dawn of the Dead began as an intended sequel to *Night of the Living Dead*, and reputedly grew out of the same unpublished three-part short story written by Romero in the 1960s (famously inspired by Richard Matheson's 1954 novel *I Am Legend*) that had also been the basis of *Night*. In chapters one and two, I trace the expansion of *Dawn* from this much darker original treatment to its lighter, more satirical, 1977 shooting script. The generic influences on *Dawn* range from E.C. Comics to the films of Robert Altman, and Romero worked within the generic tradition of apocalyptic horror and science fiction (as first characterised by Susan Sontag, Charles Derry and Robin Wood, amongst others), just as he did for much of his career, while also challenging it in significant ways, as these chapters discuss.

CARNIVALESQUE IN THE FILMING OF *DAWN OF THE DEAD*

The satirical, 'bawdy' tone of *Dawn* developed as filming got underway at the film's central location, Monroeville Mall. The atmosphere of the mall itself contributed to the comic aspects of *Dawn* often improvised by cast and crew during the long shoot. Chapter three documents the ways in which Romero and his company created a sense of carnivalesque in the shooting of the film. Christine Forrest Romero described the filming process as "a big adventure".[17] George Romero himself has said that "I tried to make it as much fun as I could for people"[18] Director of Photography Michael Gornick confirmed that Romero would listen to ideas from anyone, "he makes you a part of it, because you want so much to be a part of it".[19] And according to make-up effects maestro Tom Savini, the atmosphere in the mall was "Halloween every night. We were doing stunts, having a blast, making people laugh in this playground. I couldn't sleep. Life was so boring compared to being on the set of *Dawn of the Dead.*"[20]

At first, Romero stuck closely to his detailed script whose "very pedantic kind of structure" functioned as the kind of parable that Romero claimed to favour in his treatment of sci-fi horror themes. Filming in the mall took place during the winter of 1977; Romero and his crew closed down production during the Christmas period, by which time they had almost covered the screenplay well enough to edit together the movie as scripted. Romero reportedly used the downtime to put together a rough assembly of the picture. It was at this point that *Dawn of the Dead* seems to have taken on a life of its own. As previously mentioned, Romero apparently decided to continue shooting to add extra material to the film. Despite attempting to give *Dawn of the Dead* a different tone to its predecessor, *Night of the Living Dead*, the script was still harsh, bleak and unremitting. But this was at odds with the pop-kitsch atmosphere of the Monroeville Mall itself and the emerging fantasy element of the scenario that a number of production personnel have since observed was trying to get out in the film.

Much of this new material featured in the motorcycle gang sequence at the end of the film. The custard-pie fight between the gang and the zombies, which was not in the script, is just one example of improvisation during this second, looser part of the shoot.

Other new sequences not in the screenplay but filmed by Romero used the mall's potential to highlight the consumerism satire aspects of the story. These included the scene of Stephen (David Emge) proposing to a sceptical Fran (Gaylen Ross) in one of the mall restaurants while Peter (Ken Foree) mourns the dead Roger (Scott H. Reiniger); more shots for the montage sequence showing the four survivors reaping the spoils of the mall after wiping out all the zombies inside it; and extra footage of the zombie-filled mall itself, emphasising its vastness and almost futuristic sense of unreality. It was in this second part of the shoot that Romero and his company made *Dawn of the Dead* into "a romp, but with this underlying message that society's going to hell".[21]

According to Christopher Sharrett, a major aspect of apocalypticism in '70s horror cinema is "the tendency to expose and debunk the codes of genre film, to suggest that genre conventions are built on false assumptions of a now-dead social order, and that myth itself has been destroyed".[22] Chapter three also explores ways in which *Dawn* deconstructs the horror genre, with, as the aforementioned IMDb critic The Red Duchess puts it, "tones, modes, genres all colliding, the 'reality' or 'integrity' or, even, 'seriousness' of the film (is) as much in question as the modern world the protagonists live in… by the end we're not sure whether we're watching a horror, a comedy, a thriller, a Western, or a very bitter joke."[23] Romero's strategy, as I discuss, is very much a part of the revisionism of genre and American history in popular culture that was taking place in the 1960s and '70s.

In a sense, we might see *Dawn of the Dead* as Romero's commentary on the apocalyptic horror film cycle itself, as it stood in 1977 when *Dawn* was written. Romero was clearly a keen observer of the film industry and of the horror genre; *Dawn of the Dead* assimilates what came before it, and serves as a culmination of 1970s apocalyptic horror. More to the point, it offers a position of departure.

In their analyses of the apocalyptic horror film, Robin Wood and Christopher Sharrett identified the taboo on imagining alternatives to a socio-political system that "can be exposed as monstrous, oppressive, and unworkable but which must nevertheless not be *constructively* challenged".[24] As Sharrett puts it: "the constraints of dominant culture allow for abject pessimism but not for suggestions of revolutionary programs of change".[25]

Dawn of the Dead has an ending that differs from the one written in the script, one more optimistic than that Romero originally envisaged. Partly this was the result of a realisation on Romero's behalf that he did not necessarily have to restore normality in order to allow his protagonists to survive. What's more, however, is "the potential", as Romero has commented, "of a new kind of family",[26] and with it a cooperative society, proposed by Romero's conclusion: *Dawn of the Dead* poses tentative ways forward for humanity, a glimpse at possible new ways of living, beyond apocalypse. As such, the ending of *Dawn* suggested, for some critics, "future directions for a genre trapped in a nihilistic blind alley".[27] Romero himself would follow these future directions in his later films in the *Dead* series, and in the unproduced screenplay he wrote for 1985's *Day of the Dead*.

The filming process – and Romero' improvisational approach in the latter stages of the shoot – ended up enhancing his vision for *Dawn of the Dead*, turning it into an exuberant pop-fantasy-with-a-message. But Romero pushed *Dawn* into excess in other ways also, and these would have a big impact on the film's distribution. Chapter four will explore the impact that *Dawn*'s two hour-plus running time would have on the industry.

DAWN OF THE DEAD'S EPIC LENGTH

Romero had problems finding a distributor who would be prepared to take the picture with the running time he initially intended. With the extra material added to the rough cut, the movie clocked in at 139 minutes during its first public screenings, which caused concerns for potential distributors, who thought it much too long for an exploitation movie. But Romero refused to cut *Dawn* down to the standard exploitation movie length of 90 minutes. This caused some distributors to walk away immediately, but arguably contributes to the film's epic quality. (To an extent, *The Exorcist* [1973], in terms of budget and running time, had previously challenged the industry notion that the epic approach should only apply to historical drama, melodrama and science fiction.) Romero mounted a campaign for longer running times in movies, challenging industry norms with his own films (*Martin* originally existed in a 150-minute cut, while *Knightriders* [1981] would clock in at 146 minutes). In *Dawn*'s case, Romero argued that reducing the running time below two hours would mean removing characterisation and atmosphere and losing a lot of the film's texture, and he held out against distributors' demands.

Dawn's long running time is the reason why the film now exists in a 119-minute European version that is different to both Romero's original 139-minute "Director's Cut" (AKA "Cannes Cut") and the 126-minute Theatrical Version eventually released in America. Laurel's contract with Dario Argento and Alfredo Cuomo stipulated the delivery of a film no longer than two hours. Over two hours, and the distributor had the right to make cuts to the picture to reduce the running time. When Laurel delivered the first print of *Dawn* to their Italian co-producers, the distributor Titanus (to whom Argento and Cuomo had pre-sold their rights) demanded that these cuts be made. Argento himself set about doing so, in consultation with Romero, who was busy at the time trying to get US distribution. As Romero remarked in 1983, "basically what he took out was some of the gag lines, the character humour that he thought idiomatic to the States".[28] (Several different versions of the film were eventually distributed internationally, including a 155-minute fan edit ["The Extended Mall Hours Cut"] put together in 2001 using material from every available version and released in the US as a bootleg DVD. The proliferation of different versions of the film is another area of excess that *Dawn* explored, and a further indication of its hubristic quality as a cult film.)

Negotiations began with three potential American distributors: Warner Bros, American International Pictures (AIP) and a smaller independent, UFD. But a further area of excess was the film's graphic gore, which the distributors worried would result in the film being given an "X" by the Motion Picture Association of America. The implications of this are examined in the book's chapters on distribution (chapter four) and censorship (chapter six).

DAWN OF THE DEAD'S GRAPHIC VIOLENCE AND THE MPAA

In the USA at the time, an "X" rating was associated with pornography, and most mainstream movie distributors wouldn't touch "X" rated films for that reason. Romero submitted *Dawn* to the MPAA in 1978, and was advised that unless most of the violence and gore was removed it would be rated "X". (Romero would, in fact, campaign against the "X" rating of non-pornographic films, and addressed the National Association of Theater Owners in April 1979, calling for a new rating for films devoid of sexual content.)

Romero and producer Richard P. Rubinstein were forced to make a tough decision. They could make drastic cuts to get an "R" (which would greatly increase their chances of major distribution) or they could sidestep the ratings system altogether and release the film unrated. The latter option would limit how widely the film could be distributed and also restrict the advertising (as some theatres and newspapers refuse to advertise unrated films) but Romero's strong vision would remain intact. Despite protests from the three interested distributors, Romero and Rubinstein went with the latter option. Rubinstein tried to convince Warners, AIP and UFD that the decision to put the film out unrated made good business sense because the film's shock and gore would generate strong word-of-mouth long after the spend on advertising had stopped. As it turned out, he was right, but even so, neither Warners nor AIP were willing to release *Dawn* unrated, as chapter four discusses.

To demonstrate that there was an audience for the film, Rubinstein decided to hold a preview screening of *Dawn* in New York. He rented the Olympia Theater on Broadway West 107th Street for one night, and took out a small advert in the *New York Times*. With only minimal advertising, the preview screening sold out. The overwhelming reaction of the audience to the uncut, unrated film convinced distributors that *Dawn of the Dead*, in its extreme version, had the makings of a box-office hit. "We showed up there that night and the mob was all the way up the street," Romero recalled in interview. "We showed the film and it blew the roof off. People went crazy. People were screaming and yelling. It was incredible, the best audience experience I'd ever had."[29] As a result of the screening, Rubinstein made a deal with UFD who, on the strength of the audience reaction, agreed to put the film out uncut and unrated. It was a vindication of Romero's extreme cinematic vision: *Dawn* would go on to gross over $55,000,000 at the worldwide box office, doing well in America, Italy, Japan, Germany and Britain.

Romero has long held that the shock factor of *Dawn*'s extreme gore is an integral part of the film's satire, a cinematic 'custard pie in the face of the audience'. However, as chapter five explores, Romero was harshly criticised by many critics (including Janet Maslin and Pauline Kael) who felt that *Dawn* "desensitised" viewers to violence, and international censors were not kind to *Dawn*. In Ontario, Canada, 13 minutes were taken out by the censors in an attempt to rein in *Dawn*'s excesses. And in Australia, *Dawn* was initially banned. But it is the treatment of *Dawn* by the BBFC in Britain that makes for the most revealing case study of the film's censorship, as will be discussed in the book's sixth and final chapter.

DAWN OF THE DEAD'S RE-EDITING BY THE BRITISH BOARD OF FILM CLASSIFICATION

Romero maintained that it is because of the film's satirical humour that James Ferman (then Secretary of the BBFC) reversed the Board's original decision to make 55 separate cuts to *Dawn* totalling over two minutes of screen time. The BBFC had originally viewed Dario Argento's version, which, as mentioned previously, lacked the intentional humour of Romero's cut, but when the UK distributor (Target International Pictures) sent Romero's version instead, Ferman (in Richard Rubinstein's words) saw the satire in the film and said, "I now understand – there is a rationale for this violence," and took out only 30 seconds.[30]

The BBFC's own account, taken from their archives, goes quite differently. According to them, Ferman himself recut the film to create a version that would be acceptable as a UK "X" (now "18") certificate. In a letter to Target, he told them: "a tour de force of virtuoso editing has transformed this potential reject from a disgusting and desensitising wallow in the ghoulish details of violence and horror to a strong, but more conventional action piece… The cutting is not only skilful, but creative, and I think it has actually improved a number of the sequences by making the audience notice the emotions of the characters and the horror of the situation instead of being deadened by blood and gore.'[31]

In some ways, perhaps Ferman was right: the BBFC-edited version of *Dawn* (released in the UK in June 1980 as *Zombies: Dawn of the Dead*) is slicker and faster-paced; and reducing some of the gore actually heightens the impact of the make-up effects that remain. But, in censoring the film in this way, was Ferman also blunting *Dawn*'s anti-consumerism message? Although Romero himself didn't seem to think so at the time, telling *Starburst* that "as far as I'm concerned the intention or texture of the film hasn't been affected at all",[32] it is interesting to note that one of the sequences most affected by the BBFC cuts is the shopping mall massacre, where Fran, Stephen, Roger and Peter slaughter the zombies in order to claim the mall as their own: a scene that the script indicates is meant to create a sense of disgust at the actions of the humans in their bid to indulge their appetite for consumer goods at all costs. Although this sequence has been fully reinstated in recent UK DVD releases of the film (since 2003, *Dawn* has been passed by the BBFC fully uncut), the censoring of *Dawn of the Dead* by the BBFC on its initial UK release suggests that Romero's satire of American consumer-capitalism was ideologically troubling to the censors.

But censorship tampering through the years has not diminished *Dawn of the Dead* as "superschlock". The film continues to resonate, as the many zombie-themed films and TV series (including the hugely successful *The Walking Dead* [2010-2022]) inspired by Romero's extreme vision show. Listen carefully, and above the sounds of the relentless hordes of the living dead, their moans and shuffling feet, you may still hear strains of "The Gonk".

FOOTNOTES

1. George Anderson, "Dawn of the Dead – a Movie En-'grossing' in Every Way", *Pittsburgh Post-Gazette*, May 8, 1979, 17.
2. Alan Jones, "George Romero", *Starburst*, no. 46, August, 1982, 34.
3. Ibid.
4. Roger Ebert, "Interview with George Romero", *Chicago Sun-Times*, April 29, 1979.
5. The Red Duchess, "Review of Dawn of the Dead", *IMDb*, January 10, 2001, accessed June 9, 2020, https://www.imdb.com/review/rw0158598/?ref_=tt_urv.
6. Dan Yakir, "Morning Becomes Romero", Film Comment, Vol 15, no. 3, 1977, reprinted in Tony Williams, ed., *George A. Romero: Interviews* (Jackson: University Press of Mississippi, 2011), 50.
7. Erich Fromm, "The Nature of Violence." *The Collier's 1969 Year Book, Covering the Year 1968*. (New York: Crowell- Collier Educational Corporation, 1969).
8. Source: *American Rhetoric: Top 100 Speeches*, accessed June 9, 2020, https://www.americanrhetoric.com/speeches/jimmycartercrisisofconfidence.htm.
9. John Hanners and Harry Kloman, "The McDonaldization of America: An Interview with George A. Romero", Film Criticism, Vol 6, no. 1, Fall 1982, reprinted in Williams, *George A. Romero: Interviews*, 90.
10. "X-ed out", *Pittsburgh Post-Gazette*, Sep 30, 1980, 21.
11. Vincent Canby, "Screen: Exurban Horror: A Community Takes on Army in 'The Crazies'", *The New York Times*, March 24, 1973, 20.

12. Jones, "George Romero", *Starburst*, 36.

13. Robin Wood, *Hollywood from Vietnam to Reagan* (New York: Columbia University Press, 1986, reprint 2003), 107.

14. Source: *Rotten Tomatoes*, 'Dawn of the Dead', accessed June 9, 2020, https://www.rottentomatoes.com/m/1005339_dawn_of_the_dead.

15. A. Loudermilk. "Eating 'Dawn' in the Dark: Zombie desire and commodified identity in George A. Romero's 'Dawn of the Dead'". *Journal of Consumer Culture*, Vol 3, no. 1 (2003): 83.

16. Braddock as the "suburb" setting for *Martin* has particular associations with decay and decline (see discourse around *Out of the Furnace*'s [2013] production, mayoral term of John Fetterman, etc.). Braddock and Monroeville, despite being near one another, have very different connotations/associations. Monroeville is generally more middle class (lower- and middle-) in character, while Braddock is/was resolutely working class, and visibly impoverished even during the period of *Martin* and *Dawn*'s production.

17. Perry Martin, *The Dead Will Walk*, 2004. DVD extra.

18. Ibid.

19. Ibid.

20. Ibid.

21. Martin, *The Dead Will Walk*.

22. Christopher Sharrett, *Apocalypticism in the Contemporary Horror Film: A Typological Survey of a Theme in the Fantastic Cinema, Its Relationship to Cultural Tradition and Current Filmic Expression*, unpublished PhD. thesis, New York University, 1983, 2.

23. The Red Duchess, "Review of Dawn of the Dead", *IMDb*.

24. Wood, *Hollywood from Vietnam to Reagan*, 142.

25. Sharrett, *Apocalypticism in the Contemporary Horror Film*, 55.

26. Richard Lippe, Tony Williams, and Robin Wood, "The George Romero Interview, Toronto Film Festival, September 15th, 1979". *Cinema Spectrum* 1 (1980), reprinted in Williams, *George A. Romero: Interviews*, 63.

27. Tony Williams, *Hearths of Darkness: The Family in the American Horror Film* (Madison, NJ: Associated University Presses, 1996), 154.

28. Tony Crawley, "The King/ George Conversations", *Starburst*, no. 55, March 1983, 29.

29. Martin, *The Dead Will Walk*.

30. Paul R. Gagne, *The Zombies That Ate Pittsburgh: The Films of George A. Romero* (New York: Dodd, Mead, 1987), 97.

31. Source: "Case Study: Dawn of the Dead", *BBFC*, accessed June 9, 2020, https://www.bbfc.co.uk/case-studies/dawn-dead.

32. Jones, "George Romero", *Starburst*, 36.

CHAPTER 1: "UPSETTING THE APPLECART": CONCEPT AND GENRE

ROMERO'S ORIGINAL THREE-PART STORY

George A. Romero's inspiration – directly or otherwise – for his initial trilogy of *Dead* films, including *Dawn*, had been the novel *I Am Legend*, written in 1954 by Richard Matheson. According to Romero, he had, at some point in the 1960s, written a short story loosely based on Matheson's novel that was "a socio-political allegory of a revolutionary society overthrowing the operative society".[1] The first section of the three-part story had formed the basis of the screenplay of *Night of the Living Dead*, and parts two and three would provide the nuclei of both *Dawn* and its 1985 follow up, *Day of the Dead* (with elements finding their way into Romero's later trilogy, *Land of the Dead* [2005], *Diary of the Dead* [2007] and *Survival of the Dead* [2009]). In other words, this unpublished, untitled short story, based on the Matheson novel, would prove to be the well-spring of Romero's entire *Dead* series. Before going on to examine the narrative presented in the short story and its role in the development of Romero's ideas for *Dawn*, it is worth briefly addressing here the alleged influence of *The Last Man on Earth* – the 1964 film adaptation of *I Am Legend* – on *Night of the Living Dead*, and therefore on *Dawn* and the other films that followed. A number of commentators have speculated that a screening of *The Last Man on Earth* on Pittsburgh television in the 1960s may have sparked the idea for *Night of the Living Dead* in Romero's mind. This raises questions about the validity of Romero's claim to have written a short story based on Matheson's novel, and even whether such a short story actually existed (or was invented by Romero after the fact in attempt to assert his authorship of the story premise).

According to Bill "Chilly Billy" Cardille, the host of "Chiller Theater", a popular late-night horror show that played on WIIC-TV, Channel 11 (later WPXI-TV) from 1963 to 1984, the crew of *Night of the Living Dead* was directly inspired by a screening of *The Last Man on Earth* on his show. As he told *Fangoria* in 1986: "George Romero was in town with his production company [Image Ten] to make a film – and this is what I heard from him later. They were watching Vincent Price in *The Last Man on Earth*, and they said, 'Let's make a Chiller Theater movie. We can make a movie that's better than what they have on the air'.'[2]

The Chiller Theatre schedules published on Cardille's own website (http://chillertheatermemories.com/) list the screening of *The Last Man on Earth* as taking place on June 10, 1967.[3] This coincides with the shooting of *Night of the Living Dead*, which, according to a number of sources, took place between June and December that year. While it is feasible that Romero and his co-author John Russo wrote the script of *Night of the Living Dead* quickly and from scratch after *The Last Man on Earth* screening, accounts differ on the actual writing process of the screenplay. As Paul R. Gagne describes in his excellent book, *The Zombies that Ate Pittsburgh*:

> Romero first presented the idea for *Night* to his Image Ten partners after spending a weekend writing a screen treatment for roughly half the film… According to Romero, Russo took it over when shooting began, and that it was completed during production based on further discussions. Russo maintains that a *finished* script was ready *before* shooting began, and that he took over more as a matter of keeping the ball rolling so that shooting wouldn't be delayed.[4] [Italics in the original text.]

So, while it is *possible* that Romero had sought out Matheson's novel (or not) after the screening of *The Last Man on Earth* in June 1967 and then written a three-part short story based on it, from which he then selected the first part to develop into a screenplay for *Night of the Living Dead*, this sequence of events seems unlikely given the short time span involved. What is more, Romero claimed to have written the short story "a couple of years" before *Night of the Living Dead*, as he told Gagne in 1985:

> It always was [a trilogy], in my mind. There were always three parts to the story. They weren't dominant. All three parts were at the farmhouse. The third part was just a paragraph or two. It was a story I wrote before I ever started to write the *Night* screenplay; a couple of years before that. I started to take the first part of it and turn it into a screenplay.[5]

Romero had in fact first mentioned the short story in 1972 in an interview with Alex Ben Block conducted in the same year as Russo split with Latent Image, the commercial company he had formed with Romero and Russell Streiner. Romero and Russo co-owned the literary rights to *Night*. However, Streiner and Russo started to develop their own sequel to *Night of the Living Dead* in 1972 after the split with Romero. According to Gagne, as Romero and Russo had written the screenplay for *Night* together, this presented a legal dilemma in terms of who owned the sequel rights that was not resolved until a formal agreement was worked out in 1978 when distribution of *Dawn* sold to UFD. Was the short story that Romero claimed to have written before *Night of the Living Dead* part of his bid to assert sequel rights? Gagne describes the short story in detail in *The Zombies That Ate Pittsburgh*, but this appears to be based on a verbal account of it given to him by Romero. I contacted Gagne to ask if he was able to confirm the existence of the short story. Gagne replied: "Romero himself was the only person ever to describe the short story to me in an interview, and never produced a copy of it, stating that it was 'probably in a box in the attic' or something to that effect."[6] John Russo has, according to Gagne, insisted that the short story is, in fact, a myth, "a fabrication on the part of Romero and Richard Rubinstein to establish a claim on the living dead series as an intellectual property for the purpose of doing sequels".[7] At the time, Russo was involved in writing *The Return of the Living Dead* (1985). Ultimately the lawyers representing both parties worked out an agreement granting sequel rights to both Romero *and* Russo, with Romero using "the Dead" and Russo using "the Living Dead" in their respective titles. But why would Romero continue the short story claim given that he and Russo had worked out the dispute over sequel rights? "What I suspect," Gagne told me in correspondence, "was that the short story was something Romero had talked about so often in interviews that to him, it kind of became its own truth."[8]

Neither does the short story document appear to be amongst Romero's papers held by the University of Pittsburgh as part of their George A. Romero Archival Collection (the curator of which, Benjamin T. Rubin, informed me that much production documentation has been retained by Rubinstein, who owns the rights to *Dawn*).[9] I am therefore unable to verify whether or not the short story actually exists, or ever existed.

To a greater extent, of course, whether the short story exists or not (or when it was actually written if it does exist) is by the by; as is the role that *The Last Man on Earth* played in the conception of *Night* and Romero's subsequent *Dead* films beyond inspiring the basic plotline and certain imagery (such as the siege on the farmhouse in *Night*). What is of concern here is the influence of Richard Matheson's novel on Romero's thinking about apocalyptic horror and his approach to it in the *Dead* series. The notion of a story in three parts may well have come to Romero as his thinking on the *Dead* films and his allegorical use of apocalyptic horror developed over time. (John Russo has, in fact, rejected the claim that it was always Romero's intention to make a trilogy, stating that *Night* was "a one-off, that's all".)[10]

In 1977, Romero told *Film Comment* that what prompted him to write the short story in the first place was because he "got very much into the socio-political through-line" of the novel,[11] but was also frustrated by it because he felt that Matheson didn't follow through on the social commentary, which, as Romero saw it, was about a revolutionary society rising up to replace the existing social order. Romero later expanded on his reasons in interviews he gave in 2008, around the time of *Diary*, which was a reboot of the original story:

> I thought *I Am Legend* was about revolution. I said if you're going to do something about revolution you should start at the beginning. I mean, Richard [Matheson] starts his book with one man left; everybody in the world has become a vampire. I said we got to start at the beginning and tweak it up a little bit.[12]

The short story, as related by Romero, used flesh-eaters in the place of vampires as its central metaphor: a revolution coming into being in the form of a zombie society, with people returning to life as soon as they die to attack the living. The first part of the story (which formed the basis of *Night of the Living Dead*) dealt with the zombies first appearing and – despite the ensuing chaos and confusion – an operative society manages to stay on top of the uprising. In the second part of the story there is an equal balance between zombies and humans, with the outcome of the conflict between them undecided. The third part sees the zombies finally outnumbering the humans, turning society full circle. In Romero's original concept the three stages are all set in a farmhouse, with three different stories, featuring different characters, taking place at different times. In the first, a group of survivors take refuge in the farmhouse, and – as in *Night* – all end up eaten. Then a few months later, a human militia turn up at the farmhouse picking off the living dead, trying to control the outbreak, but the zombies themselves begin to remember how to use weapons. We cut to a number of years later, and an army of gun-toting zombies kill off the last remaining humans: the zombie revolution is complete. However, to quote Romero, the third part of the short story existed only as a "paragraph or two" (according to researcher Adam Charles Hart, Romero expanded the third part of the story to a five-page film treatment in 1979, in order to have something tangible to copyright as part of a three-picture deal with UFD), outlining Romero's intended thematic statement: that the zombie revolution does not change the dominant values of our society. "The zombies are the new masses," Paul R. Gagne writes in *The Zombies that Ate Pittsburgh*, "but they serve the same master."[14] As Romero described to *Film Comment* in 1977:

> I have this vision of a layered society where the humans are little dictators, down in bomb shelters, and they fight their wars using zombies as soldiers. The operative humans have to be out feeding the zombies, controlling them and keeping law and order. In that layer of society we'll ultimately get our hope; those are the characters we'll be able to care about. It's a return to what the zombie was in the beginning: Lugosi always lived in a castle while the zombies went out to pick the sugar cane.[15]

(The idea that a rebel faction within the human survivors would provide hope for humanity is one to which Romero would return in his unproduced screenplay for *Day of the Dead*, written in 1985, and in *Land of the Dead* – see chapter three.) Romero would further refine his thematic statement in later interviews, before committing his ideas (in modified form) to film in the *Dead* series that followed *Dawn*. Circa 1982, as Romero was starting to prepare what was originally planned to be the final film in the trilogy, *Day of the Dead*, he appeared as a guest on *Lyceum*, an arts chat-show aired on WQED-TVS PBS in Pittsburgh. Interviewed by Mary Rawson, Romero discussed the themes of his *Dead* movies in these terms:

> [The zombie films] really deal with one society swallowing another society, in this case literally... And, hopefully, over the course of the three parts of the story, which I have thought of always as a trilogy, we'll find out that it really doesn't change things, because it's kind of come back to the way they were anyway; that revolution hasn't meant all that much.

What is fascinating is that Romero could have finished his answer there, but feels compelled to go further, even though he hesitates as he struggles to formulate his thoughts before fully committing himself:

And that the fear of being swallowed up by some new societal order has not... that we have this irrational fear of it....It's very hard, we could do twenty minutes on this... We have irrational fear of being swallowed into a new order with new thoughts and new ideas. And that's really what worries us the most. It's kind of just the fear of the unknown coming, you know?[16]

Christopher Sharrett has written of the apocalyptic horror film that it "momentarily inoculates the spectator with criticisms of a failing dominant order, but then reneges on this criticism by denying that there is any worth in carrying this critical process through to a conclusion".[17] If we see Romero's statement as a willingness to confront these deep-seated cultural fears of revolutionary change, then we might therefore argue that he was prepared to attempt a significant departure from the nihilism of apocalyptic horror in his films. As he commented in 2008:

[zombies] don't represent, in my mind, anything except a global change of some kind. And the stories are about how people respond or fail to respond to this. That's really all they've ever represented to me... They are a global disaster that people don't know how to deal with.[18]

APOCALYPTIC HORROR

With *Dawn of the Dead*, then, Romero was working within – and to an extent challenging or subverting – the conventions of the apocalyptic horror film. In his seminal 1979 essay, "The American Nightmare", Robin Wood considers the American horror film, alongside the revisionist Western, to have entered its apocalyptic phase in the late 1960s–early 1970s, reflecting the ideological crisis and destabilisation that beset America during the time of the Vietnam War and leading to Nixon's resignation following the Watergate scandal in 1974. For Wood, the apocalyptic horror film of the time

obviously expresses despair and negativity, yet its very negation can be claimed as progressive: the apocalypse, even when presented in metaphysical terms (the end of the world), is generally reinterpretable in social/political ones (the end of the highly specific world of patriarchal capitalism). The majority of the most distinguished horror films, especially in the '70s, are concerned with this particular apocalypse. They are progressive in so far as their negativity is not recuperable into the dominant ideology, but constitutes, on the contrary, the recognition of that ideology's disintegration and its untenability, as all it has repressed explodes and blows it apart.[19]

Wood argues that this negation of dominant ideology, as presented by the apocalyptic horror film, made the '70s horror film one of the most progressive genres of that decade, "even in its overt nihilism – in a period of extreme cultural crisis and disintegration, which alone offers the possibility of radical change and rebuilding".[20] However, the horror genre as a whole, according to Wood, "carries within itself the capability of reactionary inflection, and perhaps no horror film is entirely immune from its operations". Further, Wood identified the genre in the '70s as moving characteristically toward an unresolvable and usually unrecognised dilemma: that the monster is the genre's true "hero".[21] These apparent contradictions within the horror genre have, as we have seen, prompted other critics to describe horror films of the 1970s as "a genre trapped in a nihilistic blind alley". Indeed, Christopher Sharrett locates the apocalyptic horror film within a broader tradition of apocalypticism in art and culture, one which insists on the "criticism of despair":

> Society is shown to be entering into or on the verge of calamity, but a way out of calamity is never in evidence. It is useless to learn from history; the power of love is extinct; social institutions have lost their mandate… despair and the wish dream of destruction are strong characteristics of apocalypse, even with those artists grappling with the issues of transcendence and social transformation.[22]

In her seminal 1965 essay, "The Imagination of Disaster", Susan Sontag had already argued that science fiction/horror films ultimately provide inadequate responses to major socio-political issues: while the concerns they raise might be valid, their conclusions tend to be formulaic and unsatisfactory. Referring specifically to cold war science fiction films of the late 1950s–early 1960s which addressed fears of impending nuclear apocalypse, Sontag commented that whilst these films reflected world-wide anxieties, they also served to allay them. Their "unremitting banality" helps to normalise "what is psychologically unbearable", thereby inuring us to the inconceivable terror of apocalypse. "They inculcate a strange apathy concerning the process of radiation, contamination and destruction," wrote Sontag. "There is a sense in which all these movies are in complicity with the abhorrent."[23]

Interestingly, in 1982, *Film Criticism* sought Romero's response to Sontag's criticism of the genre as "inadequate" in its dealing with serious concerns. Romero was guarded in his reply, as he often was at that stage in his career when pressed on the artist's responsibility toward social change. "We have to speak in terms that are recognizable and understandable," he answered. "And I don't think it has to be realistic or contemporary to do that. In fact, I think you have the reverse."[24] Later in his career, Romero would become more openly critical of the genre, and emphasise his own desire to challenge its conventions. He would refer several times to the genre in terms of "upsetting the apple cart", such as this comment he made in 2008:

> My biggest complaint about horror or fantasy is, [if] you do it to upset the apple cart, to upset the ways of the world, and then in the end, you restore it all. Well, why did we go through all that in the first place?[25]

Romero has expressed his commitment to working within the genre precisely because its formulaic nature can be easily disrupted. For Romero, the simplicity of the genre makes it adaptable to social commentary. As he told Dennis Fischer in 1999:

> I think damned near anything you want to say, you can say it in genre. It's much easier because you can be a little more obvious, you don't have to be quite as eloquent. You can make anything happen that you want to happen, so you can illustrate almost any point. I just think it's great. It's like parables, those little tales in the Bible. I think you could pick out anything, any scene that intrigued you or you felt passionate about, and figure out a way of telling it in a fantastic manner.[26]

This, of course, returns us to Romero's comment that *Dawn of the Dead* is nothing more than "superschlock", a combination of the sci-fi/monster flicks that Romero grew up watching in the 1950s. The spectre of nuclear apocalypse is apparent in all of Romero's *Dead* films; his very real fear of the Bomb during childhood informs their imagery and themes. It is no surprise that he spent his formative years, at the height of the Cold War, afraid of imminent nuclear attack. Romero admits that with the constant fear in the 1950s of "the bomb about to explode in my head, I was a pretty worried kid!"[27]

Romero's films, and those of a number of other North American directors working in the horror genre of the 1970s, can be seen as variations of the 1950s sci-fi movies that they watched as children, in their outward projection of atomic age fears. In the '70s, apocalyptic horror films arguably employed the story telling formula of 1950s sci-fi/horror disaster movies, adapting it to contemporary concerns. We might include amongst such titles *The Omega Man* (1971), *Rabid* (1976), *Invasion of the Body Snatchers* (1978), *Blue Sunshine* (1978), *Shivers* (1975), *The Crazies* (1973) and many others.

One of the first film critics to identify the "horror of Armageddon" as a major subgenre of the modern horror film was Charles Derry. In his 1977 study *Dark Dreams*, Derry surveyed American horror films made between 1960 and 1976, and found three prevalent themes in modern horror cinema: horror of Armageddon being one (the others being "horror of the personality", à la *Psycho* [1960], and "horror of the demonic" cf. *The Exorcist*). In regard to tracing the lineage of '70s apocalyptic horror (Derry uses the term "horror of Armageddon" in a similar sense to Wood's "apocalyptic horror", denoting films that depict the "end of the world" as meaning the collapse of a modern capitalist society), Derry identifies Hitchcock's *The Birds* (1963) as a key progenitor. According to Derry, "horror of Armageddon" films utilise a specific three-part thematic structure derived from *The Birds*: (1) proliferation; (2) besiegement; and (3) annihilation. Interestingly, Derry also attributes these structural themes to the work of playwright Eugene Ionesco, creating an implicit link between the modern apocalyptic horror film and the Theatre of the Absurd: "the obvious similarity between Ionesco's *oeuvre* and the horror of Armageddon is testament to the relevance of both".[28] Derry makes a number of comparisons between Ionesco's play *The New Tenant* (1953) and *The Birds*: "structurally they are the same; starting from banality, moving gradually to the extraordinary, and inexorably to the horrific…the emphasis is on the besiegement of one area (the room, the house across Bodega Bay), although we hear reports that other areas are under similar attack. In both, the inexplicably of the proliferation creates the horror."[29] These similarities also invoke comparisons between Ionesco's work and *Night of the Living Dead*; Derry claims that *The Killing Game*, written by Ionesco in 1970, bears an "astounding resemblance" to Romero's film.

Indeed, the three-part thematic structure that Derry claims is common both to Ionesco's plays and "the horror of Armageddon", is clearly applicable to *Night of the*

Living Dead, in which the first part of the narrative is concerned primarily with the increasing number of living dead gathering outside the farmhouse. This proliferation motif is crystallised in one shocking moment that takes place early in the film when Ben drives an attacking zombie out of the house: as the zombie staggers backwards through the door, Romero reveals more zombies in the background advancing towards the camera in a diagonal formation – suddenly there is no longer one but many. As the zombie numbers increase, and Harry and the other characters emerge from the cellar, *Night* then emphasises the besiegement motif: they are now trapped inside the house by the zombie masses and must fight their way out. Finally, after a failed escape attempt, the film moves inexorably into its final stages: that of annihilation. (R.H.W. Dillard, in a perceptive early analysis of *Night*, concluded that much of the film's horror arose from the film's total surrender to the fear of death. "The plot is one of simple negation," he wrote in 1973, "an orchestrated descent into death in which all efforts toward life fail."[30])

Whilst he pinpoints the primacy of *The Birds* and links the horror of Armageddon via Ionesco to the Theatre of the Absurd (both ultimately convey "the quandary of a civilization"), Derry locates the roots of '70s apocalyptic horror in the atomic survival films of the 1950s–60s, in such movies as *On the Beach* (1959), *The World, The Flesh, and The Devil* (1959) and *Panic in the Year Zero* (1962). He traces one film in particular as the earliest example of these: *Five*, made in 1951. *Five* may well be the first feature film to deal with a post-apocalyptic theme. Indeed, Derry argues that *The Thing from Another World* (1951) and *Five* are the two archetypal American horror/science fiction films of the 1950s, as "each dealt specifically with a major horror science-fiction theme: *The Thing* with the idea that there exists life on other planets that could threaten life on earth and *Five* with the idea that the earth could be virtually destroyed by the atomic age."[31] Whilst *The Thing from Another World* has gone on to become considered a science fiction classic, *Five* is all but forgotten. However, as Derry argues, "the mythic patterns of *Five* are by now very familiar to us", and the film is worth examining briefly here, particularly in relation to Romero's work.

THE POST-APOCALYPSE PRIMACY OF ARCH OBOLER'S *FIVE*

The nuclear apocalypse scenario of *Five* is a precursor to such later works as *On the*

Beach, Panic in the Year Zero, and *The World, the Flesh and the Devil,* as well as to the allegorical cold war sci-fi "radiation movies" of the 1950s (*Them* [1954], *Tarantula* [1955] and *The Incredible Shrinking Man* [1957], amongst others). The film's motifs – a small group of survivors band together after nuclear war, and begin the slow, painful process of rebuilding – certainly extends to nuclear war films of later decades such as *The Day After* (1983) and *Threads* (1984), as well as providing the post-apocalyptic "survival scenario" for numerous science fiction and horror films to come. *Five* has been praised as a ground-breaking independent production and an inspiration for the French New Wave. It was shot by Oboler and a crew of recent USC film school graduates for a reported $75,000, using Oboler's own house as the main location. Columbia Pictures picked *Five* up for distribution, but more nuclear apocalypse films would not be produced until the end of the 1950s. It should be noted that the decade was not short of atomic attack civil defence films presented on television as public information films; these, of course, focused on surviving the immediate effects of nuclear attack, but did not raise the question of long-term survival of the human race in the aftermath of such an attack, how many people might survive, and how they would cope.

Five's storyline involves five survivors of an attack that appears to have wiped out the human race but left the basic infrastructure intact. The survivors comprise of a pregnant woman and four men. In Derry's words, these are the nucleus who must "somehow continue civilization". In the process, they must come to terms with what they have lost, even as they face an uncertain future. *Five* poses questions about what the new society should be like, and whether it should attempt to preserve the values of the destroyed civilisation; values which, the film suggests, led to the destruction of civilisation in the first place.

The influence of *Five* (through its establishing genre tropes) on Romero's *Dead* series, including *Dawn*, is marked. The film shares Romero's abiding theme of "insanity" that began in *Night of the Living Dead*, with characters operating on various levels of insanity that are clear only to themselves. For example, the woman, Roseanne (played by Susan Douglas Rubeš), similarly to Barbra (Judith O'Dea) in *Night*, is traumatised into a near-catatonic state by the attack, from which she does not fully recover until the very end of the film. Political themes that critics have attributed to Romero, such as the repudiation of individualism and racism, are also present. The film suggests that cooperative social

Social satire: Monroeville shopping mall in Dawn of the Dead.

endeavour is the key to a new society. *Five*'s conclusion is that the characters must put the past behind them in order to survive, and those unable to let go of the values of a defunct society will perish. This is dramatised in Roseanne's return to the city to find that her husband has died in the blast, and the death of her unborn son, a symbol of her old life which is now over. She learns to forget the past, and start again in a brave but barren new world.

Oboler's willingness to imagine a world beyond apocalypse marks *Five* as a surprisingly radical vision, one that goes further than many subsequent films in envisaging a new world order based on the rejection of obsolete social values, taking its criticisms of a failing social order towards a logical conclusion. Indeed, *Five* arguably transcends later films like *The Birds* or *Night of the Living Dead* in terms of its willingness to go beyond nihilism. Moreover, *Five* suggests that certain themes which we might attribute to Romero are, in fact, inherent to the genre itself; Romero has merely appropriated them, recognising their continuing relevance in later decades. To his credit, Romero has acknowledged that debt to the genre many times (especially in ascribing *Dawn* as "superschlock"): "There aren't any real new thoughts, certainly no solutions, and not even any new questions in my films. I've just tried to get an underbelly into them all, maybe more consciously than some other people."[32]

If *Dawn of the Dead* – like *Five* – represents a rare and uncharacteristically adequate (or at least optimistic) response to social issues, as I believe it does, then the key to that lies within Romero's treatment of the themes. Working in the fantasy genre, how does one avoid giving "inadequate responses"? Romero's solution was to push *Dawn* towards social satire. This would eventually take him into areas of excess as he drove the concept to its logical conclusion.

It is worth noting that the moves Romero made toward a more optimistic response to the social issues presented in his films have had impact on subsequent horror cinema. Whilst Romero's optimism is rare, it is possible to nod to later films that also hinted at a brighter future. One thinks of, for example, *Shaun of the Dead* (2004), whose creators Simon Pegg and Edgar Wright are huge fans of Romero. A snippet of the score from *Dawn* appears at the very start of *Shaun of the Dead*, and it has the comedy element, but by the end of the film, there is some restoration of pre-apocalypse equilibrium, a nod to a future that isn't all bad.

AMC's *The Walking Dead*, by contrast, provides an interesting case study of rebuilding following apocalypse, which may challenge the inadequacies of apocalyptic horror. Much scholarship has been done on the subject of patriarchy and hypermasculinity in the series. But what of renewal? Does *The Walking Dead* challenge the wish fulfilment of modern post-apocalyptic as described by Sharrett? Does it offer any solutions to the impending real world apocalypse? Derived largely from Romero's vision, *The Walking Dead* appears to present the metaphysical apocalypse (the end of the world), in social/political terms, concerned as it is with the end of the world of patriarchal capitalism, and as such it offers a critique of American democracy. The question constantly facing the survivors is one of communalism. Is it possible to organise in groups of federated communes without sinking into tribal violence? How should such groups be led? How to prevent the rise of despots? Can social values of the past be redesigned to fit this brave new world or must they be rejected as defunct? Such is the urgency of these themes that *The Walking Dead* has spilled over in franchise series and thinly-veiled knock-offs such as the video game series and TV show *The Last of Us* (2022-). Their proximity arguably presents evidence of there being a cyclical return to the prevalence of the themes that I have discussed previously. Given later ways in which I connect *Dawn of the Dead* to prescient issues/

concerns in the future, this, I believe, makes the case for the film's continued relevance.

FOOTNOTES

1. Quoted in Christopher Koetting, "They're Coming to Get You, Barbra", *The Dark Side*, no. 191, March 2018, 22.

2. Roger Berrian, "Chilly Billy Remembers", *Fangoria*, no 53, May 1986, 54.

3. Source: "Chiller Theatre 1967", *Chiller Theatre Memories*, accessed June 9, 2020, http://www.chillertheatermemories.com/1967.html.

4. Gagne, *The Zombies That Ate Pittsburgh: The Films of George A. Romero*, 25.

5. Paul R. Gagne, "George Romero on Directing 'Day of the Dead'", *Cinefantastique*, Vol 15, no. 6 (1985), reprinted in Williams, *George A. Romero: Interviews*, 101.

6. Gagne, email to the author, November 20, 2020.

7. Ibid.

8. Ibid.

9. Benjamin T. Rubin, email to author, May 13, 2020

10. Quoted in Martin Coxhead, "Night of the Living Dead", *Starburst*, no. 46, August, 1982, 42.

11. Yakir, "Morning Becomes Romero", *Film Comment*, 47.

12. Mariana McConnell, "Interview: George A. Romero on 'Diary of the Dead'", *Cinema Blend*, January 14, 2008, accessed June 9, 2020, https://www.cinemablend.com/new/Interview-George-A-Romero-On-Diary-Of-The-Dead-7818.html.

13. Adam Hart & Benjamin T. Rubin – *It Came From the Archives! Unearthed Treasures from the George A. Romero Archival Collection*, (webinar), University of Pittsburgh, February 9, 2021.

14. Gagne, *The Zombies That Ate Pittsburgh: The Films of George A. Romero*, 148.

15. Yakir, "Morning Becomes Romero", *Film Comment*, 47-48.

16. Source: "Lyceum", WQED-TVS, date unknown, accessed June 9, 2020, https://www.youtube.com/watch?v=H6gCzq2IYIQ.

17. Sharrett, *Apocalypticism in the Contemporary Horror Film*, 13.

18. McConnell, "Interview: George A. Romero on 'Diary of the Dead'", *Cinema Blend*.

19. Wood, *Hollywood from Vietnam to Reagan*, 170.

20. Ibid., 76

21. Ibid., 170

22. Sharrett, *Apocalypticism in the Contemporary Horror Film*, 13.

23. Susan Sontag, "The Imagination of Disaster" in *Against Interpretation and Other Essays* (New York: Farrar, Straus & Giroux, 1966), 225.

24. Hanners and Kloman, "The McDonaldization of America: An Interview with George A. Romero", *Film Criticism*, 100.

25. Larry Getlin, "Return of 'Living Dead.'" *The New York Post*, May 18, 2008, accessed June 9, 2020, http:// www. nypost.com/ p/ entertainment/ movies/ item_ GOZg54FUU8WNmSsP5eBk9N.

26. Dennis Fischer, "George Romero on 'Bruiser', Development Hell and Other Sundry Matters", in Williams, *George A. Romero: Interviews*, 132.

27. Gagne, *The Zombies That Ate Pittsburgh: The Films of George A. Romero*, 9.

28. Charles Derry, *Dark Dreams 2.0: A Psychological History of the Modern Horror Film from the 1950s to the 21st Century* (Jefferson, NC: McFarland, 2009), 60.

29. Ibid., 62.

30. R.H.W Dillard, "Night of the Living Dead: It's Not Just Like a Wind That's Passing Through" in Gregory A. Waller, ed., *American Horrors: Essays on the Modern American Horror Film* (Chicago: University of Illinois Press, 1987), 23.

31. Derry, *Dark Dreams*, 56.

32. Gagne, *The Zombies That Ate Pittsburgh: The Films of George A. Romero*, 5.

CHAPTER 2: "COMIC-BOOK TYPE HUMOUR AND EXTREME STAGING": SCRIPT DEVELOPMENT

THE ORIGINAL TREATMENT

According to an article in *Rolling Stone* from March 1978, Romero first got the idea for *Dawn of the Dead* in 1973 at the same time as he formed a partnership with Richard Rubinstein. "I wrote a little sketch about it and put it in a drawer while I did some other things," Romero told reporter Chet Flippo.[1] This timeline would place Romero's first sketch for a sequel to *Night* as coming soon after *The Crazies*, which as Flippo notes, "Romero feels was a prototype for *Dawn*". A number of pieces have been written on *The Crazies* and its place in Romero's filmography alongside the *Dead* series, so a brief mention of it will suffice here.

As Robin Wood observes, *The Crazies* came almost exactly half-way between the two *Dead* films and is closely related to both in terms of "its confirmation of Romero's thematic concerns and the particular emphasis it gives them". According to Wood, *The Crazies* moves out "from *Night*'s concentration on the family unit into a more generalised treatment of social disintegration (a progression *Dawn* will complete)".[2] Concerning the effects on a small Pennsylvania town of an accidental release into the water supply of a bacteriological weapon that drives people mad, *The Crazies* is Romero's most explicit statement on the theme of insanity in the population (as previously mentioned in relation to *Five*): "The basic premise being that everyone in the world is operating at some level of insanity."[3] Romero first discussed this theme in relation to *Night*, when in 1972 he told Alex Ben Block, "The story (of *Night*) was an allegory written to draw a parallel between what people are becoming and the idea that people are operating on many levels of insanity that are clear only to themselves."[4] Romero's linking of social conditioning to insanity in *Night* and *The Crazies* would become key to *Dawn* (where the characters struggle to assume autonomy and self-awareness, having been contaminated by consumer greed). In other words, in Romero's films insanity is indistinguishable from ideology. Also present in *The Crazies* is Romero's distrust of authority: as in *Night* and *Dawn*, failure of authority only serves to worsen the crisis. As Tony Williams concludes: "*The Crazies* presents a frightening vision still relevant today about governments lying

"Everyone in the world is operating at some level of insanity": Roger (Scott H. Reiniger) turns psychotic in Dawn of the Dead.

to its citizens and even planning to exterminate them should circumstances demand it… the film presents an apocalyptic vision of a society in the process of collapse from which its more conscious survivors must remove themselves physically and mentally."[5] Clearly, then, *The Crazies* was still fresh in Romero's mind as he began to conceive of *Dawn*, and it is a fascinating example of the continuity and progression in his work and his thinking, even if the director himself maintained that there were no intentional similarities between *The Crazies* and *Dawn*.

"The only reason we made *Dawn of the Dead* was that George was ready to make it," Rubinstein told *Starburst* in 1983. "We spent five years resisting being categorised as a horror director since *Night of the Living Dead*, and the next five years were spent putting together the deal."[6] After the initial box-office success of *Night*, Romero was approached by distributors early on to make a sequel, but declined offers. "We had people saying could we have the next one ready in two weeks."[7] At that point, *Night* was regarded as an exploitation B-picture, and Romero assumed that its success would be shortlived: "Initially it went out and played drive-ins and neighbourhood theaters and in six months it was gone."[8] By then Romero had moved on to make *There's Always Vanilla* (1971), an attempt to cash in on *The Graduate* (1967) and *Goodbye Columbus* (1969) (although the film is probably closer in spirit to the New York independent film movement of the time cf. *David Holzman's Diary* [1967], *Greetings* [1968], *Putney Swope* [1968]) and the ill-fated proto-feminist witchcraft movie *Season of the Witch*, AKA *Hungry Wives*, AKA *Jack's Wife* (1973). Romero maintained that he was "afraid that making (the sequel) back-to-back would not be artistically satisfying" and that this was another reason why he resisted making a sequel to *Night* for so long.[9] He was also, early in his career, clearly reluctant to become typecast as a horror director, as he told *Starburst*: "[R]ight after that film I went through a paranoia which had nothing to do with the genre but with the realisation of what business was like in the States by being characterised in such a limiting way. It took me a long time to get used to the fact that they would treat me like a horror film director regardless."[10]

By 1970, *Night* had become critically acclaimed in Europe, and was on its way to being canonised in America, with repertory screenings at the Museum of Modern Art, the Waverly Theatre in Greenwich Village and the Elgin Theatre in Chelsea, New York, where it became a "midnight movie". American film critics, including Roger Ebert, who had previously dismissed *Night* as a grade-Z movie without merit, now began to consider it an important film with a significant social subtext. As Romero's reputation grew with critics in France and in the UK, his own perception of his audience, it seems, began to change in subtle ways. Romero may have felt that social commentary was expected of him. In an interview with A.V. Club in 2008, he stated: "[E]ven though I always felt that maybe a little too much was being said about [*Night*], I was also influenced by what was being said. Time comes to make a second film, I resisted, didn't have an idea, couldn't think of anything… I felt the sequel had to live up to these huge expectations."[11] However, he was also acutely aware, following the disappointments of *There's Always Vanilla*, *Jack's Wife* and *The Crazies*, of the needs of the box office. This dilemma seemed to inhibit him when it came to the question of a sequel. As he recalled in 2008, "I almost froze up [and thought] if I'm going to do a sequel or another one, I'm going to have to be socially conscious, and it became an obsession."[12][13]

There was, however, a pressing reason for Romero agreeing to a sequel. By 1973, he was floundering both creatively and financially. His partnership with Rubinstein at Laurel Tape and Film (formerly Laurel Productions of Pennsylvania), making sports documentaries for syndication and importing foreign movies for US distribution, helped Romero regain his business footing and produce the critically acclaimed *Martin*, but, as Romero revealed to *The Pittsburgh Press* in 1979, "I was struggling, so I began to think seriously of it."[14] A sequel to *Night* made good business sense at that point in Romero's career. In 1976, Laurel had bought back the rights to *The Crazies* from the original distributor, Cambist, and was having "increasing success booking it into cult theaters across the country";[15] another way, perhaps, that Romero might have considered *The Crazies* as a prototype for *Dawn* – in terms of a business model trading off the reputation of *Night of the Living Dead*. Also, the proposed Russo-Streiner sequel to *Night* may have spurred an initially reluctant Romero to work on his own sequel as a necessary commercial move.

In interviews, Romero has claimed that as he started to think about a possible sequel to *Night*, he revisited his original short story idea of setting the whole three-part narrative in the farmhouse, and began to rework it. He told *Rod Serling's The Twilight Zone Magazine* in 1981: "[W]hen I started to make *Dawn*, I decided to change that. The phenomenon of the zombies is continuing – it's expanding, in fact – so I decided that I didn't want to keep it at the same location."[16] Russo's proposed sequel, *The Return of the Living Dead*, which the author published as a novel in 1979, was intended as a direct continuation of the first film in terms of storyline and tone. It made sense, then, for Romero's sequel to be its own film, with a different attitude and feel to *Night*. Again, it is *The Crazies*, rather than *Night*, that provided the prototype. Romero was conscious of developing his comic-book style as a filmmaker at this stage in his career. He considered *Night* to be a collaborative effort between the partners of Latent Image/Image Ten; *There's Always Vanilla* even more so. Romero claims to have felt creatively stifled at times by the democratic nature of these productions, with only short sections of *Night* that he felt reflected his own emerging filmmaking personality. *Jack's Wife* had suffered from under-budgeting that had affected its form: much of it resembles a made-for-television movie, with flatly filmed dialogue scenes. Whilst *The Crazies* also suffers from talky sequences, Romero felt that it was more successful in showcasing his visual strengths as a director. As he told Gagne in 1986, "it came close to representing, for the first time, my filmmaking personality. It's the first film that a viewer might be able to identify as mine based on its style."[17]

There was also the issue of the changing times. Five years had passed since *Night of the Living Dead*. Critics had read into the film commentary on the breakdown of the nuclear family, American Civil Rights struggles and the war in Vietnam. Like most artists, Romero wanted to find an approach that was relevant to the "now", to capture the zeitgeist. At the same time, he felt the need initially to retain the claustrophobic horror that had made *Night of the Living Dead* successful as a genre movie. "I wanted a surface texture that would provide for small confined spaces while also reflecting on what America is becoming – a sterile, fast-food society. At first I wasn't sure how to convey that idea."[18]

As he was playing around with all these concepts in his head, whilst struggling with a case of writer's block brought on by the expectations placed upon him by critics, Romero was introduced to the Oxford Development Company's shopping mall in Monroeville, thirty miles outside of Pittsburgh. Mark Mason, one of the Company's owners, and a friend of Romero, invited him on a tour of the mall, including the Civil Defence area and crawlspaces above it. Mason revealed to Romero that he had always had this fantasy about a hermit living up there, someone who could have the pick of anything he wanted from the mall below. The proverbial light-bulb went off in Romero's mind. "That gave me the idea that was the perfect setting for the equal balance part of the trilogy."[19] The mall would provide a microcosm, serving the same purpose as the farmhouse in *Night* for the developing apocalypse, with the sequel depicting the cusp of the phenomenon, "where we feel the zombies will take over because they have the mall at the end. By the end, the mall looks just the way it does during the day."[20]

Opened in 1969, the 1,130,000-square-foot Monroeville Mall was exactly the kind of cathedral of consumerism that Romero would describe in his script for *Dawn* as one of the "great symbols of a consumer society".[21] Inside the two-storey enclosed mall were 126 speciality stores, plus a Gimbels, Joseph Horne Company, G.C. Murphy's and, in the central forecourt, a J.C. Penney's (which would feature prominently in the film). Fully climate controlled, the mall also included tropical gardens, a fountain court, another court with a two-storey high cuckoo clock, an Olympic-sized ice skating rink, a pharmacy, a bank, four movie theatres and several restaurants and eateries.

Large indoor shopping malls like Monroeville Mall, built in the suburbs, were a relatively new phenomenon in 1973, and it is difficult now to imagine how much of a novelty they must have seemed to Romero at the time. Certainly, no film had used a shopping mall the size of Monroeville as its main location at that point. Later, malls would feature in movies as a way to depict the everyday life of suburbanites (especially in teen movies of the '90s). "I'm really surprised no one else picked up on the idea," Romero told *Rolling Stone* in 1978, "because now there are these shopping developments where you can live on top and work and shop down below and never have to leave the building."[22] By the time *Dawn* was produced, the idea had, in fact, been used in two key horror films of the 1970s, although neither focused exclusively on the mall as a setting. David Cronenberg featured a sequence where mall shoppers, fleeing a virus-infected madman, are gunned down by armed guards in *Rabid* (1977) (whilst his earlier *Shivers* used as its main location a modern residential complex, a commodified living-work-shopping space similar to the mall of *Dawn*).[23] Jeff Lieberman's *Blue Sunshine* stages its final showdown in a Los Angeles shopping mall, in which the bald-headed showroom dummies could easily be mistaken for zombies. In these films, too, the shopping mall symbolises a new age of rampant consumerism that exerts a dehumanising influence on the characters.

Romero sat down and wrote his initial sketch of the idea, that he later developed into a treatment "which was short and incomplete",[24] and, as he told *Film Comment*, "was very heavy, ponderous, possessing roughly the same attitude as *Night*".[25] The original treatment for *Dawn* centred on a couple, a man and a pregnant woman named Steve and Francie, survivors of the zombie outbreak, living in a crawlspace above the mall and occasionally venturing down for supplies and food. The male functions as the hunter-gatherer getting supplies from the stores below. As Romero told Paul R. Gagne in 1986, "they were really like cave-people; they were naked all the time… It was too dark. It was really ugly."[26] Even though Romero would come to rethink the starkness of the initial treatment, he was already taking the material into areas of extremity, stating to Gagne that he was "really going out there" in trying to make the story uncompromising. In his original hand-written synopsis, dated April 1974, Romero states: "[W]e see Steve and Francie living in a series of stark, white rooms, sparsely furnished, but scattered with food and medical supplies, games, a large calendar on the wall… The two are obviously under great strain… perhaps they make love violently as a release of their tensions… We learn that it is almost time for Steve to leave on some mission. Francie doesn't want him to go, but he must as they need more supplies."[27]

According to Gagne it was at this point in 1974 that Romero also started to think about a third film and found that he was going too far into the final stage of the zombie story. The initial treatment features a subplot in which the military is feeding the zombies (the story begins with the discovery of trucks carrying human remains that are to be frozen as food for the zombies) and the zombies are controlled by a one-eyed stranger who appears to have "some telepathic command over the creatures".[28] "I had gone too far with the zombies," Romero told Gagne in 1986. "They were already being fed and trained to function as slaves, and at that point they should have just been stumbling around wondering what to do." Romero realised that he would have to spool back the story to an earlier stage in the zombie phenomenon, with this middle episode providing the fulcrum. Yet he remained reluctant to do this, and even during the filming of *Dawn of the Dead* Romero was still talking to journalists about the final stage of the story, in which "my idea to take it further is to actually have human operatives that are trying to preserve their own kind of operative situation and in fact using the zombies initially, training them to serve their own needs".[29] For Romero, the real monsters of the whole piece were the human "sellouts", the "corporate monsters" who try to exploit the zombie apocalypse for their own material gain. It is an idea that Romero would return to in his unproduced screenplay of *Day of the Dead*, written in 1985; and elements of it would feature in 2005's *Land of the Dead*.

There is a sense, then, in this first treatment that Romero wrote for *Dawn*, of him backing away from the immediate subject matter, even at the point of inspiration. Indeed, the full potential of the mall setting, and its sociological implications, did not impress itself on Romero until the filming of *Dawn* was well under way, at which point he shifted gears as he realised "that the place itself, the mall, was too funny to serve for a nightmare experience".[30] That was to be a process of discovery for Romero and his collaborators.

The initial treatment, then, was a very rough sketch that would be reworked and rethought, as Romero circled closer to his concept. By no means is the basic premise of the treatment discarded in the final film – rather, it is developed in important ways: Fran, in the film, like "Francie" in the treatment, is pregnant, and the notion of shifting gender roles is explored in much greater depth in the film itself. However, what *is* discarded is the unremitting bleakness of the treatment; this would be replaced by an increasingly bawdy and irreverent tone as Romero moved toward ever more extreme forms of social satire in the scripting and filming process.

SATIRE AND SUPERSCHLOCK

"If you want to make serious statements, I think you are better off doing them in a satirical way," Romero told Alan Jones in 1982.[31] Romero's thinking about the sequel developed significantly between his original treatment and his working draft screenplay, written in 1977. The tone of *The Crazies* – an anti-militaristic film – was one of dark irony, as was much of *Night; Dawn* would see that irony moved into extremity and therefore into satire. As Romero subsequently remarked, his extreme treatment of the subject matter actually lightened it, as humour played a greater part. Romero, in fact, considered his method a necessarily crude one, as he explained to Jones: "[T]he allegory is very frontal, very obvious and I don't think I'm saying anything that's new. Nor do I think I'm answering any questions or imposing them. I'm using the horror fantasy genre to restate the same things a lot of other people have stated more eloquently." As already mentioned, Romero came to see his films, from *Dawn* onwards, as modern day parables, moral tales delivered in popular forms. Partly this was in recognition of the needs of a genre movie audience. "In the sixties," Romero told *Film Comment* in 1977, "we used to sit around in coffee shops and talk and solve all the problems of society and filmmakers did it in their movies. We don't do that anymore. Films are still critical of society, but this criticism has taken the form of parables communicated through the fantasy film."[32] Romero was almost certainly thinking about his younger self when he talked about the coffee shop intellectual, and to an extent his earlier films, *There's Always Vanilla*, and *Jack's Wife*, were attempts at earnest social criticism that failed to find an audience. "If I was trying to write social criticism in that way I might possibly have a readership of twenty or thirty and be hanging out in Greenwich Village somewhere. I have the best of both worlds. I love popular form cinema… and I think that more craftsmanship goes into it on many levels than goes into, so called, serious cinema."[33]

By 1977, Romero had, in fact, very clear ideas about the aims of his cinema, how to incorporate allegory and use satire: "I do it in very broad strokes, with a comic-book type humour and extreme staging and a very pedantic kind of structure… the socio-political parable is to me like a handshake with the audience… it's a wink and should be taken as such."[34]

For Romero, "fantasy has always been used as parable, as socio-political criticism…I love the Japanese Godzilla films. They're not scary at all, but as a phenomenon born out of the war, the bomb, they say more to me than *Hiroshima Mon Amour* (1959). So I insist on having that underbelly."[35] In talking about "comic-book type humour and extreme staging", Romero is almost certainly referencing E.C. Comics, which he grew up reading in the 1950s, alongside watching B-movies. The ghoulish satire of *Dawn* is firmly in the E.C. tradition.

Romero himself has said that what he – alongside Stephen King – took from E.C. was "the irreverence and uninhibited presentation".[36] Tony Williams elaborates on this in comparing Romero's stylistic choices to the E.C. tradition of graphic imagery and transgression of cultural taboo. (Romero has also referred to his work as Grand Guignol in relation to its graphic imagery, and I will discuss this in more detail later in this book.) E.C. has been praised for its socially conscious, progressive themes that anticipated the American Civil Rights movement and 1960s counterculture. Williams claims that E.C. provided "alternative and subversive imagery to a youthful world reacting against materialism and Cold war conformity" and that E.C. offered "culturally satirical antidotes to the hypocritical conformism of the era".[37] Comics like *Shock Suspense* engaged in social criticism that was considered un-American, condemning militaristic patriotism and lynching. Many E.C. stories included shock endings that often involved decaying corpses rising from their graves, or ironic gruesome twists that served as poetic justice for their characters. As such, E.C. contained moral elements, as Williams notes: "They demonstrated the dangers of injustice and oppression to anyone considering such criminal paths." Romero uses poetic justice motifs often in his films (although not necessarily influenced by E.C. in this respect). One thinks of the grimly ironic fates suffered by Roger and Stephen in *Dawn*, who succumb to material greed and die because of it (but not before turning into zombies first). E.C. wasn't afraid to mock its readers who revelled in the gruesome irreverence of stories, in a similar way to Romero, who described *Dawn* as "a pie in the audience's face".[38] The satire of E.C. was aimed squarely at its readers, to whom it referred as "boils and ghouls". Romero claimed the comic-book violence of *Dawn* satirises that kind of audience.

In his use of satire, Romero has almost certainly been influenced by other directors whom he admired. Asked in 1982 to name his favourite directors, he cited Fred Zinnemann, John Schlesinger and Ken Russell, with Stanley Kubrick as his "main man".[39]

Romero was no doubt thinking primarily of *Lolita* (1962), *Dr. Strangelove* (1964), *2001: A Space Odyssey* (1968) and *A Clockwork Orange* (1971) (he was not a fan of *The Shining* [1980]). *Strangelove*, in particular, provides an interesting comparison with *Dawn*: Kubrick had originally conceived of it as a serious drama, before realising that the premise of nuclear apocalypse was so absurd that a more truthful statement on the subject could be made through black humour. Kubrick thus took *Dr. Strangelove*, as he did a number of his other films, into areas of extremity as a satire, as would Romero with *Dawn*.

Anti-military satire, of which *The Crazies* is an example (and *Dawn* also satirises America's obsession with guns), was a popular trend in cinema at the start of the 1970s, starting with Robert Altman's *M*A*S*H* (1970). Romero may well have looked to Altman, too: a fiercely independent filmmaker who bucked Hollywood trends; a master social and political satirist. Altman was well-known for incorporating improvisation in his films, and may have inspired Romero to have added unscripted sections to *Dawn* in the second part of the shoot in an attempt to "pull all the stops out,"[40] as I discuss in the next chapter.

Romero was a keen observer of the horror film, and would watch the movies of his contemporaries in the genre. Certainly he was familiar with the work of David Cronenberg and Wes Craven, both of whom he admired. Of Cronenberg's films he particularly liked *The Brood* (1979) and *Scanners* (1981); he praised Craven's *The Hills Have Eyes* (1977) for its uncompromising approach, describing it as a film that "doesn't apologise for what it sets out to do and has a lot of energy behind it".[41] He was aware of the excesses of the genre in the '70s, telling Alan Jones: "In the last ten years we've seen some pretty extreme stuff, *The Texas Chainsaw Massacre* (1974), *The Last House on the Left* (1972), *Night of the Living Dead*, actually, for what it represented at the time… you have to say, 'Ok, that's how far we've come, if we are going to extremes, let's exercise it.'"[42] It's interesting that Romero includes his own film amongst the cycle. In the four years between getting the idea for a sequel to *Night of the Living Dead* and actually writing the screenplay to *Dawn*, the horror genre had evolved considerably. Romero was acutely aware of this and understood the developments. We might actually see *Dawn* not only as a continuation of Romero's own work, and homage to the B-movies and E.C. comics of his youth, but as a conscious appropriation of the tropes and themes that had become prevalent in the genre following *Night of the Living Dead*. Furthermore, Romero not only adopted the extremity of the horror genre in the 1970s, he aimed to "exercise" it also. The 1977 working draft of *Dawn of the Dead* thus represented an extreme vision that would become even more so during filming.

FOOTNOTES

1. Chet Flippo, "When There's No More Room in Hell: The Dead Will Walk The Earth", *Rolling Stone*, March 23, 1978, 48.

2. Wood, *Hollywood from Vietnam to Reagan*, 104.

3. Sam Nicotero, "Romero: An Interview with the Director of 'Night of the Living Dead'", *Cinefantastique*, Vol 2, no. 3 (Winter 1973), reprinted in Williams, *George A. Romero: Interviews*, 18.

4. Alex Ben Block, "Filming 'Night of the Living Dead': An Interview with Director George Romero", Filmmakers Newsletter, Vol 5, no.3 (January 1972), reprinted in Williams, *George A. Romero: Interviews*, 8.

5. Tony Williams, *The Cinema of George A. Romero: Knight of the Living Dead* (London: Wallflower Press, 2003), 73.

6. Tony Crawley, "Richard P. Rubinstein on Romero", *Starburst*, no. 46, June 1982, 37.

7. Jones, "George Romero", *Starburst*, 37.

8. Beth Accomando, "George A. Romero Interview", KPBS, February 6, 2008, in Williams, *George A. Romero: Interviews*, 160.

9. Quoted in Christopher Koetting, "No More Room in Hell:, The Dark Side, no. 193, June 2018, 16.

10. Jones, "George Romero", *Starburst*, 38.

11. Noel Murray, "Interview: George Romero", A.V. Club, December 2, 2008. Accessed June 26, 2020. https://film.avclub.com/george-romero-1798213286

12. Accomando, "George A. Romero Interview", KPBS, 160.

13. Indeed, following an early meeting with American International Pictures where it was suggested that Romero make *Dawn of the Dead* with a Black cast to cash in on the then-current "Blaxploitation" craze, Romero indicated that he was agreeable to the idea. In a letter to Richard Rubinstein, dated April 1974, (courtesy of The George A. Romero Archival Collection, University of Pittsburgh), Romero explains how lending *Night* a Black focus had attracted audiences to the film and given it social resonance: "This could be accomplished again by simply casting a Black man and woman in the roles of the humans as they appear in the existing draft.'"

14. Ed Blank, "'Living Dead' Sequel Opens Here April 13", *The Pittsburgh Press*, April 1, 1979, 131.

15. "On Screen", *Pittsburgh Post-Gazette*, May 27, 1976, 10.

16. Tom Seligson, "George Romero: Revealing the Monsters Within Us", Rod Serling's Twilight Zone Magazine, August, 1981, reprinted in Williams, George A. Romero: Interviews, 82.

17. Gagne, The Zombies That Ate Pittsburgh: The Films of George A. Romero, 56.

18. Seligson, "George Romero: Revealing the Monsters Within Us", Rod Serling's Twilight Zone Magazine, 83.

19. Yakir, "Morning Becomes Romero", Film Comment, 48.

20. Flippo, "When There's No More Room in Hell: The Dead Will Walk The Earth", Rolling Stone, 48.

21. George A. Romero, "Dawn of the Dead (working draft)", 1977.

22. Flippo, "When There's No More Room in Hell: The Dead Will Walk The Earth", Rolling Stone, 49.

23. In his excellent monograph on Cronenberg, Ernest Mathijs points out that the indoor shopping mall is a Canadian invention. See The Cinema of David Cronenberg: from Baron of Blood to Cultural Hero (London: Wallflower Press, 2008).

24. Blank, "'Living Dead' Sequel Opens Here April 13", The Pittsburgh Press, 131.

25. Yakir, "Morning Becomes Romero", Film Comment, 48.

26. Gagne, The Zombies That Ate Pittsburgh: The Films of George A. Romero, 83.

27. George A. Romero, Synopsis – Dawn of the Dead, April 1974. Courtesy of The George A. Romero Archival Collection, University of Pittsburgh.

28. George A. Romero, Treatment – Dawn of the Dead, undated. Courtesy of The George A. Romero Archival Collection, University of Pittsburgh.

29. Flippo, "When There's No More Room in Hell: The Dead Will Walk The Earth", Rolling Stone, 49.

30. Yakir, "Morning Becomes Romero", Film Comment, 48.

31. Jones, "George Romero", Starburst, 36.

32. Yakir, "Morning Becomes Romero", Film Comment, 50.

33. Jones, "George Romero", Starburst, 35.

34. Yakir, "Morning Becomes Romero", Film Comment, 50.

35. Ibid.

36. Tony Williams, "An Interview with George and Christine Romero", Quarterly Review of Film and Video, Vol 18. No. 4 (2001), reprinted in Williams, George A. Romero: Interviews, 139.

37. Williams, The Cinema of George A. Romero: Knight of the Living Dead, 18.

38. Lippe, Williams, and Wood, "The George Romero Interview, Toronto Film Festival, September 15th, 1979". Cinema Spectrum, 67.

39. Hanners and Kloman, "The McDonaldization of America: An Interview with George A. Romero", Film Criticism, 99.

40. Yakir, "Morning Becomes Romero", Film Comment, 54.

41. Jones, "George Romero", Starburst, 35-36.

42. Jones, "George Romero", Starburst, 36.

CHAPTER 3: "I KNEW THAT THE ONLY WAY TO DO THIS WAS TO JUST BEAT IT TO DEATH": PRODUCTION

THE FIRST SHOOT

At 253-pages, Romero's working draft screenplay of *Dawn of the Dead* is an extremely detailed breakdown into action and dialogue that demonstrates the kind of "Langian formal precision" that (as The Red Duchess on IMDb puts it) reins in *Dawn's* excess. Gagne describes the screenplay's attention to detail as "almost obsessive", with "pages upon pages describing bits of action and scenes that take only a few moments of screen time".[1] The screenplay is not written in the usual format of master scenes, instead Romero breaks the action down into individual shots or "beats" of the scene. It is, as Romero has pointed out, "more of a storyboard than a script". As he explained to Gagne, "in essence, the script was notes to work from. I wanted a lot of detail because I knew I was never going to have time for storyboards or anything like that."[2]

The formal precision is reflected in the screenplay's "pedantic kind of structure" that sets out the story as a conscious morality tale reminiscent of the E.C. style. The basic premise of *Dawn* can, in fact, be described very simply, like that of a comic book: "[H]ave people trying to escape the living dead, and they end up in this shopping mall, this consumer paradise."[3] Initially, during filming, Romero was very careful to stick closely to the detailed script, whose social commentary was deliberately built into the sequence of story events. As he explained to Roy Frumkes during the shoot:

> [T]here are certain things that I want to happen that build on each other: in this film the people starting to get tempted and attracted by the mall and adopting their military approach to taking it over… And those are things that I try to keep as close as possible to the script because there's a certain build that was written into the script which I really think adds to the flow of the overall suspense of the film.[4]

The story begins three weeks into the zombie crisis and society is already at the point of meltdown. As in *Night*, the disintegrating media is feeding the people misinformation and "moral bullshit". Martial law has been declared and citizens are forbidden from occupying private residences. But with no confidence in the authorities' handling of the crisis, people are disobeying orders to turn over the bodies of the dead to the National Guard. As things get worse, survivors of the zombie outbreak flee the besieged cities. We follow four of these survivors as they hole up in a giant shopping mall on the outskirts of Philadelphia. Initially, they plan to use the mall only as a rest stop before they fly off in their helicopter to find an island somewhere (the idea of finding an island to inhabit recurs throughout Romero's *Dead* films) on which to "grow vegetables and go fishing, to live in the wilderness".[5] But the survivors succumb to the allure of the mall which represents to them the false security of consumer society (as Romero comments in the 2004 documentary *The Dead Will Walk*, "the way that society has been conditioned to think that as long as you have this stuff, life is wonderful; being falsely attracted and seduced by things that really shouldn't have value in your life but do").[6]

Like the America that has been lost, the mall has to be taken from the zombies, who are its original inhabitants, just as the Native Americans originally occupied the land. In the screenplay Romero even compares the mall to the old West, with the survivors as the cowboys taking the land from the "injuns". But, after the mall is seized – amid a mass slaughter of zombies – and the survivors fully indulge their materialism, the rot soon sets in. The hollowness of their consumerism is finally brought home to them. "The group has become a family," Romero writes in the script, "with all the disadvantages of comfortable living, including the inability to communicate."[7] When a biker gang (characterised in the script as Mexican bandits) then tries to take the mall, the survivors are faced with a choice: give up the mall and flee, or fight to keep it. Essentially, the screenplay of *Dawn of the Dead* presents the message that human beings must learn to find a new way of living that breaks with destructive traditions of the past, or be destined to join the ranks of the living dead.

Romero presents an extreme vision of the consumer society that America had already become by the late 1970s. Shopping malls are vast "cathedrals", "great symbols of a consumer society", as Romero describes them in the script, "revealing the Gods and Customs of a civilization now gone".[8] There is also a dark undercurrent of racial violence that has led commentators, such as Sharrett, to read *Dawn* not only as "a comment on consumer capitalism", but also a statement on "the imperialist rampage that was the US attack on Southeast Asia".[9]

As in *Night of the Living Dead*, the nature of the apocalypse is essentially racial. In the script's early tenement sequence we are presented with a shocking vision of the racial divide facing America in the mid-1970s. As Tony Williams notes, the zombie crisis hits the poorest in society the hardest – the African-Americans, Puerto Ricans and Hispanics in low-rent tenement buildings.[10] A SWAT team, including the protagonists Roger and Peter, are sent in to evacuate the tenement and arrest the Puerto Rican insurgents led by Martinez; but the ensuing massacre is a result of the rampant racism espoused by the trooper, Wooley, who uses the crisis as an excuse to go on a rampage of hatred and bigotry.

Like the characters in *Night of the Living Dead*, Peter and Roger, and the couple Fran and Stephen, are faced with a choice: adapt or die. Essentially, *Dawn of the Dead* presents their spiritual journey towards this realization, and examines the ideologies that influence them in making those choices. Those who successfully complete the journey survive; those who do not, perish. As part of this process, there is a re-enactment of the macho power of the gun which defines the male order. Both Stephen and Fran must master the art of the gun in order to gain a place within the power structure. When the survivors first arrive at the mall by helicopter, their immediate decision is to colonise it, to exert this power. However, their reasons for colonising the mall are dubious; Romero suggests in the script that the items they pillage are "clearly not all functional. Some are representative of the luxuries considered necessary by a consumer society." Only Fran appears to recognize this; at first she tries to persuade Stephen that the mall could be a "prison". "What happened to the idea about the wilderness?" she asks him in the script. The opportunity for a new way of living that the crisis presents is initially quashed by the group who remain entrenched in their old ways; Fran's voice, as the lone woman, is for the time being discounted. The men's decision is instead to fortify the mall, symbolising their entrenchment in the old values. Fran's strength as a character slowly grows throughout the script, as her viewpoint becomes increasingly acknowledged by the men as the voice of reason. In order to find this voice, however, she must first break free of her own cultural conditioning, her reliance upon the men and the protection that they provide, and the security that the mall brings.

Underlying the urgency for ideological change is the growing realisation that the main threat to the protagonists comes from within. Increasingly in the script Romero identifies

Fran (Gaylen Ross) is the lone voice of reason in Dawn of the Dead.

the macho values of the group as an agent of infection; both Roger and Stephen become "infected" by machismo which leads to their downfall. Stephen and Roger's machismo is thus another Romero "level of insanity" on which the characters operate that is "only clear to themselves"; but it is tied to their material acquisitiveness as well. So whilst on one level the story plays on consumerist fantasies inherent in seizing the shopping mall, it also acknowledges both the absurdity and the immorality of such a response to the zombie outbreak: we instinctively know that this is not a viable option for long-term survival even when the zombies are vanquished from the mall.

Again, it is Fran who most clearly understands this. "What have we done to ourselves?" she asks despairingly. Hence, Fran learns to pilot the helicopter, a symbol of her step away from reliance upon Stephen, in favour of autonomy and self-awareness; she is able to escape her social conditioning. Stephen, however, is not. Stephen, Roger and the outlaw biker gang (and, to a degree, Peter) have internalised the violence of the American Way to the extent that they are unable to extricate themselves from it. At the end of the script (but not the film), all the characters perish because of it. The ritualistic playing out of the frontier myth in the shopping mall proves, once and for all, that the American values which led to this apocalypse, are racist, destructive and must be rejected. Survival of the human race depends upon it.

ROMERO'S ASSEMBLY DURING CHRISTMAS SHUT-DOWN

As Gagne points out, the most significant difference between the script of *Dawn of the Dead* and the finished film is one of personality. Although considerably lighter than the original treatment, "Romero's shooting script for *Dawn* is still somewhat harsh, a straight-forward outline of the film's gruesome action with none of the lighthearted, playful spirit that ultimately crept in during production".[11] Romero himself came to this realisation during the Christmas shut-down of the film, when he took the opportunity to edit together the footage shot so far, which, according to Gagne, included "a good deal of the film's main dialogue and plot framework".[12]

The three-week break gave Romero time to work with the material, most of which had been shot at Monroeville Mall. Hunched over his 16mm pic-sync editor, surviving mostly on coffee and cigarettes, Romero found the footage of the mall a revelation even as he cut and spliced it. As part of *Dawn*'s overall visual design, Romero had decided to eschew the claustrophobic light-and-shadow patterns of his previous films (notably *Night of the Living Dead*) in favour of bright light to evoke the safe, comfortable environment of the mall. As he told Gagne, "I wanted the mall to *look* like the mall."[13] But it seems that Monroeville Mall's gaudy ambience had only become fully apparent to Romero when he saw it as photographed by Michael Gornick in the dailies. This spurred a growing feeling in Romero, which intensified as he assembled the footage, that the tone of the film needed to change to reflect that of the mall itself. "When he got to the mall it had a different atmosphere than he'd already thought about *Dawn of the Dead* having," John Amplas claims in the documentary *Document of the Dead*. "The mall brought a futuristic look to the film. It was so vast."[14] Not only does the mall look futuristic in the film, its garishness makes the satire of the film implicit ("The idea of the mall itself, the moment we see it, the moment we come in and see what it is, I think it's going to become obvious in terms of what we're saying about the false security of consumer society").[15] As Romero told *Film Comment*: "I realised that the place itself, the mall, was too funny to serve for a nightmare experience. *Dawn of the Dead* is a nightmare, but it's more a pop fantasy than a brooding nightmare — which *Night*, with all its funny scenes, was."[16]

As one reads the script of *Dawn of the Dead*, one can easily picture Romero's editing, his style, and the camera angles, but it is difficult to visualise the colour and lighting designs, or what the mall looks like in the film, and as Romero came to realise, "all of those influence people's attitude towards it, as well as my own desire to lighten things up, go more action-adventure".[17] We know that Romero wanted *Dawn* to be its own film, with a different attitude to *Night of the Living Dead*, to have it "grow out of what is happening today rather than what was happening in 1968".[18] The mall's 'vibe' – its '70s pop-kitsch atmosphere – became unmistakable when seen photographed on film, and Romero ultimately decided to go with this vibe which seemed to him to speak of the times. "The picture's really designed for right now," he told Frumkes. "It's much more of a comic book, it's much lighter."[19] Thus, Romero made the decision, during that Christmas shutdown, to change the texture of the movie; in Romero's words, "to make it bawdier".[20] Romero has often used the word "bawdy" to describe *Dawn of the Dead*, and it's an interesting choice, one which evokes the carnivalesque, as I discuss shortly.

Romero was troubled that he had deliberately reined himself in as a result of *Night's* auspicious reputation, becoming self-conscious when as a filmmaker he should be letting himself fly. As he told *A.V. Club* in 2008, "a lot of the decisions I initially made [on *Dawn*] were basically me thinking 'I gotta live up to the expectations'. It wasn't until about halfway through the production that I realized that I should just fly by the seat of my pants like I did the first time…"[21]

Romero's obsession with being socially conscious, had led him to become very disciplined in the way he approached the screenplay for *Dawn*, when the subject matter, by its very nature, warranted 'excess'.

> I was trying to be as conscious as I could but I realised I was doing it without innocence. And halfway through that production I sort of shifted gears and said, wait a minute, I can really have fun with this and try and make it reflective of the times. And to make it a comment that doesn't sort of take over the thrill ride part of the film.[22]

More to the point, as he told Gagne in 1987, "I knew that the only way to do this was to just beat it to death."[23]

THE SECOND SHOOT – IMPROVISATION AND CARNIVALESQUE

Dawn of the Dead, as Romero commented to Alan Jones in 1982, "carries things to an absurd degree that we know is absurd".[24] In the tradition of what Bakhtin has called the carnivalesque, Romero ridicules the beliefs that underpin the society of its time, here the ideology of consumer-capitalism. As Gagne points out, "with gleeful irreverence, Romero suggests that *Dawn*'s zombies are the ultimate consumers, carried to the absurd extreme of consuming people".[25] The zombies themselves are carnivalesque characters: zombie nurses, nuns, insurance salesmen, softball players and, particularly memorable, a Hari Krishna. *Dawn*'s liberal, graphic gore has a distinct thematic context in this regard: "[G]arish, brighter-than-life, day-glo blood splashes all over the place as zombies tear limbs and entrails from their victims and devour them like so many hamburgers from a fast-food joint."[26]

Bakhtin relates the great carnivals of medieval Europe as occasions for social authority to be temporarily inverted. The anarchic and liberating spirit of the carnival marked a short period of time where the Church or State had no control over the lives of revellers, where set rules and beliefs could be ridiculed or reconceived, clearing the ground for new ideas to enter public discourse. Such temporary transgression during carnival may have been "licensed", but the spirit of free-thinking engendered by periods of carnival made permanent social change possible over time. Carnivalesque literature, according to Bakhtin, carries the public spirit of the medieval carnival in literary form. We might see filmmakers invoke the carnivalesque in their works of satire. Altman, for example, influenced by Fellini, featured carnival sequences in *Brewster McCloud* (1970), whilst *M*A*S*H* and a number of his other ensemble pieces like *A Wedding* (1978) and *Health* (1980) invoke the carnivalesque in their irreverent portrayals of social and political institutions.

As Romero told Roger Ebert:

> I wanted to bring out the nature of the shopping centre, the retail displays, the mannequins. There are times when maybe you reflect that the mannequins are more attractive but less real – less sympathetic, even – than the zombies. Put those kinds of images side by side, and you raise all sorts of questions.[27]

The public spirit of the carnivalesque followed through in the improvised filming that took place in the mall when production resumed there in January, 1978. In contrast to the first shoot, during which Romero had closely followed his screenplay, the cast and crew – and even the zombie extras – found themselves free to "indulge in all manner of spontaneity and improvisation".[28] In effect, Romero turned the filming *itself* into carnival. As he told Gagne in 1987: "I could have shot forever in that place! It was just *constant* invention. We'd get there and we'd wind up in front of a store, and there'd be a display, or whatever, that we'd want to use. It was so much fun – I could have just kept shooting that movie!"[29]

The carnivalesque is perhaps most apparent in the final battle sequence between the protagonists and the motorcycle raiders. Here the comedy and chaos on-screen act as a total subversion of the values of consumerism that Romero sought to satirise. As Gagne comments, the free-for-all with the motorcycle raiders turns into slapstick with custard pie and soda-water siphon attacks on the zombies.[30] Romero sends up the military-style campaign of the raiders by playing a cavalry charge bugle-call on the sound-track (earlier in the film he sends up the redneck machismo of NRA-types in a similar way). The mall muzak, used as an ironic counterpoint throughout the film, is most memorable in the absurd polka that closes *Dawn*. Indeed, the incongruity of "The Gonk" (a silly, jolly tune by British composer Herbert Chappell which often featured on UK children's television programmes in the early 1970s) over the closing credits of *Dawn of the Dead* has made it as much the film's theme music as the celebrated Goblin soundtrack (in fact, Romero met with resistance from distributors about reprising "The Gonk" over the closing credits.)

The carnivalesque spirit of *Dawn*'s second shoot infected the crew, many of whom ended up doubling as zombies or playing roles in the motorcycle gang. Tom Savini's comment that "the atmosphere was Halloween every night"[31] relates not just to his (largely improvised) role in the film as leader of the motorcycle bandits but also to the "farcical ways to kill and maim zombies"[32] that he was continually thinking up for the film's final sequence where the zombies take the mall back for themselves. Perhaps most telling, though, is the phenomenon of the zombie extras who turned up en-masse to take part. Crew members relate stories of how many of the extras were willing to do seemingly anything as zombies, including eating animal innards on camera. Romero

Colonialism: Stephen (David Emge) learns the way of the gun in Dawn of the Dead.

himself has always claimed not to understand the public's fascination with dressing up as zombies – in his own films or in the mass gatherings ("Zombie Walks") that have taken place in many American and European cities in recent years. However, a number of those who have played zombies in Romero's films have spoken publicly about the experience and the strange effect being a zombie had on them. During *Dawn*'s second shoot, a number of journalists visited the set; most of them found themselves taking part as zombie extras. *Rolling Stone*'s Chet Flippo recalled his own experience of playing a zombie in *Dawn*:

> The minute Romero yelled "action" something remarkable happened: my eyes went out of focus, my hands clenched grotesquely, and I developed a lurching gait as I went after that motorcycle. I wanted that food and I almost got it. By the time the scene was shot twice… I was out of breath and my pulse was pounding.[33]

Turning the filming of *Dawn* into carnival and encouraging constant invention from cast, crew and extras injected *Dawn* with a boisterous quality that was lacking in the script. More than that, though, it moved *Dawn* toward other genres in a self-reflexive way; one gets a sense that, by the end of the film, *Dawn of the Dead* has "deconstructed" itself. Or, at least, Romero has sought to free the film from the constraints of genre.

"The major change that's happened – from my conception upon first reading it and now – is that it's lightening up," David Emge told a documentary film crew during *Dawn's* second shoot. "When I first read it, it was awfully shocking in terms of numbers of bodies being maimed and gallons of blood being spilt, but there's a quality coming out that is counterbalancing that. It's definitely becoming more of a fantasy, more of an adventure, than I first conceived of it upon first reading it."[34]

Romero's decision to shift gears, growing from his desire to lighten the tone of *Dawn of the Dead* and "go more action-adventure"[35] is very much in keeping with the way Romero pushed *Dawn* to the limits. As he told *Film Comment*:

> I meant it to be kind of exuberant. And the battle that develops over Revlon and Charmain and whatever treasures they believe they've found takes the trappings from the traditional genre and puts it in high adventure – a mixture of weird pop with the fantastic… I'm a sucker for high adventure. The mall struck me as a high-adventure area: there are even jungles in it! And all those guns and weapons and using the car in it – it's *The Dirty Dozen* (1967) coming to Monroeville! With the action sequences in *Dawn* it was pure fun. I felt as if there were no restraints, like running free with all your senses.[36]

DECONSTRUCTION OF GENRE

Memories of the anarchic and liberating public spirit of *Dawn's* second shoot stayed with Romero when it came to make his next film, *Knightriders*, which was almost certainly influenced by his experience on *Dawn*. Indeed, the premise of 1981's *Knightriders* – in which a troupe of modern medievalists try to live by their own anachronistic moral code and not "sell-out" to the corporations – directly invokes the carnivalesque and creates a similar clash of genres to *Dawn*. Its mix of *Ivanhoe*, AIP biker movie and King Arthur legend was Romero's attempt to expose the increasing commercialisation of culture, what he saw as the ongoing "McDonaldization" of America.

Christopher Sharrett has commented on the horror genre's tendency to become increasingly self-reflexive, to deconstruct itself, "and by doing so to reflect the sense of bankruptcy of collective beliefs that have frequently been mediated in the conventions of genre film".[37] *Dawn of the Dead* presents a collision of genres, so that by the end of it "we're not sure whether we're watching a horror, a comedy, a thriller, a Western, or a very bitter joke".[38] Thereby, Romero sought to debunk white America's twin obsessions of militaristic colonialism and consumerism: the country's foundational collective beliefs. As Romero told *Prevue*: "*Dawn* had a certain viewpoint about society eating itself alive in the rush to consume material goods. We're digesting the planet on our way to a genocidal end."[39]

Running through *Dawn* is a critique of frontier mythology which compares with that of the revisionist Western films of the 1960s and '70s. This is consciously injected into *Dawn*'s script by Romero, who uses terms like "bandits" and "whoops like a cowboy" to liken the colonisation of the mall (which involves an abhorrent slaughter of zombies) to the winning of the Old West and the survivors to cowboys. The revisionist Western or "anti-Western" had a strong influence on the horror films in the "American Nightmare" cycle, which came into particular focus with *The Texas Chain Saw Massacre* and *The Hills Have Eyes*. *Dawn of the Dead* can be seen as both continuation and culmination of this shared cultural inquiry.

The atrocities in Southeast Asia and increasing opposition by Americans to the war in Vietnam prompted historical revisionism in the 1960s to acknowledge the violence inflicted on indigenous peoples, and a drawing of parallels between the massacre of the Vietnamese and the slaughter of Native American tribes in the pursuit of Manifest Destiny. As Wes Craven has noted, "Most of us grew up thinking that the Indian was the bad guy who mysteriously disappeared. We never thought we might have exterminated all indigenous nations in the United States to get their land."[40]

The revisionist Western placed the context of the Native Americans and cowboys alike in a darker setting to films of previous decades. Such works as *Soldier Blue* (1970) depicted greater moral ambiguity than presented by the traditional Western, with the distinction between "good guy" and "bad guy" less clear cut and ethics blurred. At the heart of the revisionist Western is a questioning of the racial division of civilisation/ savagery that underpinned the white settlers' belief in Manifest Destiny.

The question of colonial violence as inherent to American history was taken up in the key American horror films of the 1960s–70s. Like the revisionist Western, the horror film, as we know, is considered to have entered its apocalyptic phase during this turbulent period of civil rights struggle. The key horror films from 1968 to 1978, taking on the mantle of the revisionist Western, represent a sustained and developing inquiry into the causes of the breakdown in American society, locating its roots in the very "frontier spirit" that underlies the American Way. *The Last House on the Left* presents that there is no escape from violence in American society because violence is too deeply engrained within the culture, as much a part of interpersonal relationships as it is international politics. *The Texas Chain Saw Massacre* further develops the savagery/civilisation dichotomy of the revisionist Western to locate in the pioneer myths of the Old West the roots of a moral schizophrenia facing modern American society. Following on from that, *The Hills Have Eyes* stages a virtual re-enactment of the Pilgrims vs. Indians wars to implicate the former as the more violent of the two. *Dawn* arguably concludes the inquiry with the total rejection of the doctrine of Manifest Destiny, as the surviving characters give up their guns and return the mall to the zombies, its "indigenous peoples".

The interplay between filmmakers can be seen in the remarkable intertextuality of these films: a direct result of the cultural interaction and exchange between horror directors in their richest period of achievement. This can be partly attributed to the genre savvy of the filmmakers involved but also to their continuing sense of shared inquiry into the dark heart of the American pioneer myth, with each film building upon theme successively. One gets the sense of a baton being passed back and forth within 1970s horror – from Romero (*Night of the Living Dead*) to Craven (*The Last House on the Left*) to Tobe Hooper (*The Texas Chain Saw Massacre*) to Cronenberg (*Shivers*) to Lieberman (*Blue Sunshine*) and back to Romero (*Dawn of the Dead*) – a working through of the issues collectively, as each delves deeper into the nature of the "apocalypse" facing the society of its time.

But whereas the early films of Hooper and Craven were unwilling to move beyond the apocalyptic, the work of Cronenberg, Lieberman and Romero in the 1970s moved tentatively towards the possibility of a new social order. Cronenberg's *Shivers* offered a vision of sexual revolution based on the writings of Freudian psychologist, Norman O. Brown, that was deeply ambivalent. In its portrayal of the 1970s as a consumerist dystopia whose revolutionary ideals have been replaced by mass psychosis (zombieism), *Blue Sunshine* bridges the ideological gap between *Shivers* and *Dawn of the Dead*. All three films critique the consumer-capitalist impasse of the 1970s; and *Blue Sunshine* provides the crucial (and often overlooked) transition between the ambivalent sexual politics of *Shivers* and *Dawn of the Dead*'s tacit observation of alternative ideologies and countercultural values.

Dawn of the Dead, like *Shivers* and *Blue Sunshine*, places itself squarely in the "invasion-metamorphosis" sci-fi-horror subgenre as described by critic Andrew Tudor: "[C] ollectively, we have become potential victims, to be transformed into zombies, gibbering maniacs or diseased wrecks," writes Tudor in *Monsters and Mad Scientists: A Cultural History of the Horror Movie*. "Yet however vast its scale, the heart of this narrative lies in the emphatically internal quality of its threat. It is not simply that we may be destroyed, as we might have been by a score of traditional movie monsters. It is also that we will be fundamentally altered in the process; that our humanity itself is at risk."[41]

Intriguingly, the invasion-metamorphosis narrative that Tudor describes, perhaps because of its emphasis on human transformation as allegory of social and political change, seems to form the basis of the more optimistic horror films of the "American Nightmare" cycle. Whereas the savagery/civilisation contradiction of *The Last House on the Left*, *The Texas Chain Saw Massacre* and *The Hills Have Eyes* seems impassable – it is presented as essentially two sides of the same coin – the living/dead dichotomy in *Dawn of the Dead* is surpassable: although, admittedly, it requires a fundamental shift in the values of society, which the film suggests nothing short of a countercultural revolution can bring about. As Robin Wood noted, the zombies in Romero's films are presented as neither a reactionary or negative force nor as a "return of the repressed"; instead, Romero's strategy is that of depriving them of "positive or progressive potential in order to restore it to the human characters".[42]

THE CHANGED ENDING

Dawn of the Dead, then, can be seen as both the culmination of the "American Nightmare" cycle and a departure from the nihilism of the apocalyptic horror film. As Wood claims, it is "perhaps the first modern horror film to suggest – albeit very tentatively – the possibility of moving beyond apocalypse".[43] What makes *Dawn* remarkable in this respect is its ending, which is guardedly optimistic without restoring normative values.

The basic formula of the horror film Wood identifies as, "normality is threatened by the Monster".[44] If the resolution of this conflict between the normal and the monstrous reveals the ideological orientation of a given horror narrative, it follows that the film's ending – whether the narrative achieves closure in the form of a restoration of normality or not – is a crucial factor in determining its political implications. We might say that a typical horror narrative can end in one of three ways:

1. The monster is destroyed and the status quo restored. There is a clear sense of closure and, as Rick Worland points out, the restoration of normality is often "signaled through the formation or preservation of the heterosexual couple or family group".[45] The political implication of this type of ending is clear: normality is worth saving and dominant values should be endorsed.

2. The monster is destroyed and the status quo apparently restored, but the narrative closure is ironic, as in *Night of the Living Dead*, thus undercutting any sense of resolution of wider issues or endorsement of dominant values.

3. The monster remains un-destroyed and therefore the narrative remains open – the horror is on-going. Normality remains under threat but its basic values are shown to be worth fighting for; the monster is resolutely "Other".

Clearly, the first type of ending denotes a conservative horror narrative – the purpose of threatening normality is to restore it again, reaffirming traditional values in the process. This type of ending is often attributed (not entirely justifiably) to the "classic" 1930s–40s horror film.

The second type of ending, prevalent in the 1970s (*Deathdream* [1972], *The Last House on the Left*) can be seen as more subversive because the status quo is discredited; however no alternative to the dominant ideology, beyond a kind of nihilistic despair, is usually offered, causing some critics to question the extent to which these films can be called progressive.

The third type of ending and its variation, "the monster wins – everybody dies", arguably arose from postmodernism (it is popular for franchises) and its veneer of nihilism masks its commitment to endorsing deeply reactionary values.

It is an inherent contradiction of ideology that our culture allows for depictions of its own destruction but will not permit the envisaging of a political alternative to capitalism. There exists in the dominant culture, as Wood remarks, a taboo on imagining alternatives to a system that "can be exposed as monstrous, oppressive, and unworkable but which must nevertheless not be *constructively* challenged".[46] In the apocalyptic horror film, this translates as showing society in breakdown whilst stopping short of actually presenting any way out of apocalypse. The nihilism of the apocalyptic horror film, as Sharrett notes, presents a "criticism of despair".[47]

Filmmakers in the "American Nightmare" cycle are distinguished by their preference for non-restorative endings in the sense that, although the immediate threat by the monster to society may be fended off (or not, as the case may be), a wider crisis facing society remains. What concerns these filmmakers is exposing the conditions in society that created the monster in the first place. Therefore, restoring order remains impossible as long as those conditions persist. A clear example of this can be found in Larry Cohen's *Its Alive* (1974), which ends with the birth of another monstrous baby after the first one is killed. The film implies that whatever evil of society caused these monsters to be born has not been vanquished.

Dawn of the Dead has an ending that differs from the one originally written in the script. The ending finally committed to film is more optimistic than the one in the script, in which all the protagonists, including Peter and the pregnant Fran die. Partly this was the result of a realisation on Romero's behalf that he did not necessarily have to restore normality in order to allow his two remaining protagonists to survive.

Romero's scripted ending ran thus:

> The creatures advance on Peter. He backs away, trying to lead them from the skylight. They crash through the living space, upsetting the carefully planned room. On the roof, Fran desperately starts the helicopter engine. Peter backs into the storage room, slamming the door. The creatures approach the door and the super-gun roars one last time. The Zombies push through the door and move in for their feast. Several

zombies manage to scramble up the skylight to the roof. Fran stares, transfixed. The blades roar up to full speed. The creatures advance toward the machine. Fran steps out onto the running board; the creatures very close now. She crouches, watching for a moment, then looks up at the spinning blades. She stands straight up, driving her head into the spinning blades. A headless form falls to the roof. The Zombies advance.[48]

Indecision about the ending arose early on and remained throughout the shoot. An alternative optimistic ending, in which Peter and Fran escape in the helicopter, was apparently inserted into the script alongside the original pessimistic one. *Rolling Stone* journalist Chet Flippo reported that when he visited the set during the second shoot in January 1978 there were "two endings in the script",[49] and that the issue was unresolved until several weeks later. Some sources, including Romero, say that he shot both endings (although footage of the original ending has not yet come to light). Romero was leaning towards the pessimistic ending which he felt was in character with *Night*. As he told Gagne in 1987:

> I really pulled toward the tragic ending, but then I couldn't decide whether I was doing it just because I wanted a family resemblance to the first film. I really got lost in what I wanted. Also the effect didn't work great – it would have been spectacular to have her stand up into the blades, and I'm sure that had the effect been wonderful, I would have kept it that way. I was really on the fence with it, right down to the last. Then I just woke up one day and decided to let them go simply because I liked them too much.[50]

Despite members of the crew urging Romero "you can't kill everybody, you can't do it",[51] at first, he wasn't willing to give up the tragic ending, because he wanted to leave the "applecart" upset, and thought the pessimistic ending in the script was the best way to do that. During the second part of the shoot, as Romero and his team moved away from the script in order to work "moment by moment",[52] the general consensus became for the optimistic ending. "I think they made a great choice. There had to be some kind of uplifting ending," stated Ken Foree in *The Dead Will Walk*.[53]

Eventually, Romero came to the same realisation despite his initial misgivings:

One of the things that's always bothered me about horror is that the only reason to do it is to upset the applecart, and it seems like everybody very deliberately restores order. They shoot the giant spider and it's all over. Halfway through that film, I realized I didn't have to restore order just to have a couple of people survive.[54]

The ending of *Dawn*, although still inconclusive, offers a ray of hope for Peter, Fran, and her unborn child in that they might survive in order to start afresh. More than this, though, is the fact that Peter and Fran are able to fly off on equal terms, possibly to set up a new co-operative society based on what they have gained from their experiences: "the potential", as Romero has commented, "of a new kind of family".[55]

In a sense, the final scene in *Dawn of the Dead*, with the white woman and black man thrown together, mirrors the situation in *Night of the Living Dead*, where Ben and Barbara are forced together in the farmhouse; however, whereas that relationship was marked by distrust and suspicion, we now have mutual trust and respect. America's minorities have finally risen to take control together. *Dawn of the Dead*, as it stands, is somewhat open-ended and inconclusive, but in its tentative suggestion of a possible new social order it remains arguably the most progressive of horror films made in the 1970s.

"In *Dawn of the Dead* I think there's an optimistic perspective," Romero told *Film Comment* in 1977. "The fact that the characters, Peter and Fran, finally opt to survive, instead of just giving up, is hopeful. The devastation and the apocalyptic massacre in the mall are there, but there's also an escapist attitude through the film."[56] Looking back on *Dawn*'s uplifting ending in 2004, Romero remarked: "I love that swell of the strings when they fly away at the end. I mean, how can you live without that, man?"[57]

Writing in *Hollywood: From Vietnam to Reagan* (first published in 1986), Robin Wood details why the ending that Romero eventually chose is a radical one:

The film eschews any hint of a traditional happy ending, there being no suggestion of any romantic attachment developing between the survivors. Instead of the restoration of conventional relationship patterns, we have the woman piloting the helicopter as the man relinquishes the rifle to the zombies. They have not come very far, and the film's conclusion rewards them with no more than a provisional and temporary respite: enough gasoline for four hours, and no certainty of destination. Yet the effect of the ending is curiously exhilarating. Hitherto, the modern horror film has invariably moved toward either the restoration of the traditional order or the expression of despair (in *Night*, both). *Dawn* is perhaps the first horror film to suggest – albeit very tentatively – the possibility of moving beyond apocalypse. It brings its two surviving protagonists to the point where the work of creating the norms for a new social order, a new structure of relationships can begin – a context in which the presence of a third survivor, Fran's unborn child, points the way to potential change. Romero has set himself a formidable challenge, and it will be interesting to see how the third part of the trilogy confronts it.[58]

Dawn is necessarily open-ended. As we know, even during *Dawn's* production a trilogy was foremost in Romero's mind; as the "equal balance" part of the trilogy, *Dawn* is designed to defer resolution and deny any restoration of order. Another reason why Romero finally opted for an uplifting ending to *Dawn*, rather than replicate the pessimistic conclusion of *Night*, is because he finally shrugged off the need to live up to the expectations placed on him by that film's critical and financial success. As he told *A.V. Club* in 2008:

> I realized I should just let it ride. So, I threw in a lot more humor and had a little fun with it. Initially, when I set out to do *Dawn of the Dead*, my motives weren't innocent, because I didn't think I could ever achieve that kind of intuitive innocence of the first film, when I just said, "Whatever, I don't really give a shit if anybody sees this movie." I've never achieved that again. But I realized while making *Dawn* that I have this sort of platform, where if I feel like saying something about what's going on in the world, I can bring back the zombies and do it again. That's how I developed this franchise, or whatever it is.[59]

Dawn is therefore open-ended partly because Romero was already thinking in terms of a trilogy. The resolution was to occur in the third film. The final part of the story would illustrate that, in spite of the zombie phenomenon offering humanity the chance to start afresh, in the words of Tony Williams, "ironically, the moral is that nothing really changes at all".[60] An autocratic human regime rises up to recreate the old society, with its social divisions even more keenly drawn. However, in Romero's originally intended version of *Day of the Dead*, a rebel alliance is formed amongst a small group of outcasts who eventually topple the regime. The rebels (including a group of children) escape to an island to form a new cooperative society, and the script concludes with the revelation that the zombie plague is finally over. As Romero commented in 1977, it is in the underdog layer of human society where "we'll ultimately get our hope; those are the characters we'll be able to care about".[61] The original *Day of the Dead* script would culminate with Romero's overarching message (as he expressed it in 2005):

> [T]he zombies are this external force in my mind. It's like the story is happening in and around them and nobody's paying attention to them… In the meantime, there's this huge shift going on. And, I guess, in a distant sort of way, they represent what mankind should be and what the people should be about, that power-to-the-people thing.[62]

As he said in 1981: "The underbelly in all my movies is the longing for a better world, for a higher plane of existence, for people to get together. I'm still singing these songs."[63]

Primarily for budget reasons, Romero did not get to film his original script of *Day of the Dead*, although crucial elements of it remain in the final version and in Romero's later trilogy, particularly in *Land of the Dead* and *Survival of the Dead*. *Knightriders*, of course, was a stepping stone from *Dawn* to the original *Day* in terms of its implicit rejection of modern mainstream society. However, Romero's saga of the living dead was never followed through to its intended final conclusion that a better world is possible. One cannot help but think of the cultural pressures placed on Romero. As Sharrett has said, "the constraints of dominant culture allow for abject pessimism but not for suggestions of revolutionary programs of change".[64] These same pressures would come into play during *Dawn of the Dead*'s distribution.

FOOTNOTES

1. Gagne, *The Zombies That Ate Pittsburgh: The Films of George A. Romero*, 91.
2. Ibid.
3. Martin, *The Dead Will Walk*.
4. Roy Frumkes, *Document of the Dead*, 1980.
5. Romero, "Dawn of the Dead" (working draft, 1977), 111.
6. Martin, *The Dead Will Walk*.
7. Romero, "Dawn of the Dead" (working draft, 1977), 171.

8.   Ibid., 74-75.

9.   Christopher Sharrett, "The Horror Film as Social Allegory (And How it Comes Undone)", in Harry M. Benshoff, ed., *A Companion to the Horror Film*, (Oxford: John Wiley and Sons, 2014), 62.

10. Williams, *The Cinema of George A. Romero: Knight of the Living Dead*, 89.

11. Gagne, *The Zombies That Ate Pittsburgh: The Films of George A. Romero*, 91.

12. Ibid., 93.

13. Quoted in Gagne, *The Zombies That Ate Pittsburgh: The Films of George A. Romero*, 92.

14. Frumkes, *Document of the Dead*.

15. Romero interview in Frumkes, *Document of the Dead*.

16. Yakir, "Morning Becomes Romero", *Film Comment*, 48.

17. Romero interview in Frumkes, *Document of the Dead*.

18. Lippe, Williams, and Wood, 'The George Romero Interview, Toronto Film Festival, September 15th, 1979'. *Cinema Spectrum*, 65.

19. Frumkes, *Document of the Dead*.

20. Seligson, "George Romero: Revealing the Monsters Within Us", Rod Serling's *Twilight Zone Magazine*, 82.

21. Murray, "Interview: George Romero", A.V. Club.

22. Ibid.

23. Gagne, *The Zombies That Ate Pittsburgh: The Films of George A. Romero*, 88.

24. Jones, "George Romero", *Starburst*, 34.

25. Gagne, *The Zombies That Ate Pittsburgh: The Films of George A. Romero*, 87.

26. Ibid., 88.

27. Ebert, "Interview with George Romero", *Chicago Sun-Times*.

28. Gagne, *The Zombies That Ate Pittsburgh: The Films of George A. Romero*, 94.

29. Ibid.

30. Ibid., 94.

31. Martin, *The Dead Will Walk*.

32. Gagne, *The Zombies That Ate Pittsburgh: The Films of George A. Romero*, 94.

33. Flippo, "When There's No More Room in Hell: The Dead Will Walk The Earth", *Rolling Stone*, 46.

34. Emge interview in Frumkes, *Document of the Dead*.

35. Romero interview in Frumkes, *Document of the Dead*.

36. Yakir, "Morning Becomes Romero", *Film Comment*, 54.

37. Sharrett, Apocalypticism in the *Contemporary Horror Film*, 2.

38. The Red Duchess, "Review of Dawn of the Dead", *IMDb*.

39. Quoted in *The Dawn of the Dead Reference Page*, http://broonsbane.tripod.com/dawnmain.htm

40. Tony Williams, "Wes Craven: An Interview", *Journal of Popular Culture and Television*, Vol 8, no. 3

(1980), 12.

41. Andrew Tudor, *Monsters and Mad Scientists: A Cultural History of the Horror Film* (Oxford: Basil Blackwell Ltd, 1989), 97.

42. Wood, *Hollywood from Vietnam to Reagan*, 102

43. Ibid., 107.

44. Ibid., 71.

45. Rick Worland, *The Horror Film: An Introduction*, (Oxford: Blackwell, 2007), 21.

46. Wood, *Hollywood from Vietnam to Reagan*, 142.

47. Sharrett, *Apocalypticism in the Contemporary Horror Film*, 13.

48. Romero, "Dawn of the Dead (working draft)"

49. Flippo, "When There's No More Room in Hell: The Dead Will Walk the Earth", *Rolling Stone*, 44.

50. Gagne, *The Zombies That Ate Pittsburgh: The Films of George A. Romero*, 91.

51. Christine Forrest interview, Martin, *The Dead Will Walk*.

52. Romero quoted in Flippo, "When There's No More Room in Hell: The Dead Will Walk the Earth", *Rolling Stone*, 44.

53. Ken Foree interview, Martin, *The Dead Will Walk*.

54. Murray, "Interview: George Romero", A.V. Club.

55. Lippe, Williams, and Wood, "The George Romero Interview, Toronto Film Festival, September 15th, 1979". *Cinema Spectrum*, 63.

56. Yakir, "Morning Becomes Romero", *Film Comment*, 51.

57. Martin, *The Dead Will Walk*.

58. Wood, *Hollywood from Vietnam to Reagan*, 107.

59. Murray, "Interview: George Romero", A.V. Club.

60. Williams, *The Cinema of George A. Romero: Knight of the Living Dead*, 128.

61. Yakir, "Morning Becomes Romero", *Film Comment*, 48.

62. Stephen Applebaum, "George A. Romero: Land of the Dead", *BBC Movies*, September 19, 2005, accessed June 26, 2020. http://www.bbc.co.uk/films/2005/09/19/george_romero_land_of_the_dead_interview.shtml.

63. Dan Yakir, "Knight after Night with George Romero", American Film, May 1981, 42-45, 69, reprinted in Williams, *George A. Romero: Interviews*, 70.

64. Sharrett, *Apocalypticism in the Contemporary Horror Film*, 55.

CHAPTER 4: TOO LONG AND TOO STRONG: DISTRIBUTION

DAWN OF THE DEAD AS A 'REBEL TEXT'

In 2003, Robin Wood described Romero's first zombie trilogy – *Night, Dawn* and *Day* – as "one of the most uncompromising critiques of contemporary America (and, by extension, Western capitalist society in general) that is possible within the terms and conditions of a 'popular entertainment' medium".[1] The caveat "within the terms and conditions" suggests that Wood might place *Dawn of the Dead* (and arguably the other *Dead* films as well) in the category of "rebel text": an oppositional work within the Hollywood system. The notion of the "rebel text" in Hollywood productions is an interesting one both generally speaking and in relation to *Dawn of the Dead* – and it is one that is open to debate both generally and in the case of Romero's film as well. It bespeaks the commercial pressures placed on filmmakers working within the constraints of dominant culture.

Notions of counter-cinema and the "progressive text" or "rebel text" arose from a post-May 1968 concern with cinema and ideology. In 1969, Jean-Louis Comolli and Paul Narboni published an editorial in *Cahiers du cinéma* called "Cinema/Ideology/Criticism", which proposed a methodology by which cinema might be evaluated ideologically. This consisted of a set of cinematic categories into which individual films might be placed, based on the premise that "because every film is part of the economic system it is also a part of the ideological system" and, therefore, "every film is political, in as much as it is determined by the ideology which produces it".[2] The vast majority of movies, Comolli and Narboni argued, "are imbued through and through with the dominant ideology in pure and unadulterated form, and give no indication that their makers were even aware of the fact". At the other end of the spectrum, according to Comolli and Narboni, are explicitly political films that deal with a directly political subject and use it to attack dominant values; other films, they argued might go "against the grain" insofar as they break down traditional ways of depicting reality and therefore become political; or, conversely, remain apolitical despite their apparently political subject matter through an adherence to classical form and its adherence to bourgeois realism. Although Comolli and Narboni refer to a number of contemporary European New Wave films in relation to these first four categories, the fifth, and most complex, category relates primarily to "many Hollywood films…which while being completely integrated in the system and the ideology end up partially dismantling the system from within".[3] These are films which

> seem at first sight to belong firmly within the ideology and to be completely under its sway, but which turn out to be so only in an ambiguous manner. For though they start from a nonprogressive standpoint, ranging from the frankly reactionary through the conciliatory to the mildly critical, they have been worked upon, and work, in such a real way that there is a noticeable gap, a dislocation between starting point and the finished product… The films we are talking about throw up obstacles in the way of ideology, causing it to sway and go off course. The cinematic framework lets us see it, but also shows it up and denounces it.[4]

Critics like Wood used auteur-structuralism to untangle the ideological ambiguities of Hollywood films, arguing that "it is only through the medium of the individual that ideological tensions come into particular focus".[5] Hence, post-Comolli and Narboni scholars were able to champion certain directors – such as John Ford, Howard Hawks and Alfred Hitchcock – as progressive, despite their integration into the Hollywood system, their films constituting "rebel texts" within the mainstream.

Barbara Klinger, however, writing in 1984, questioned the relational distinction implicit in Comolli and Narboni between counter-cinema and classical Hollywood, arguing that the bedrock proposition that the progressive must exhibit "textual characteristics which are strategically reactive to commonplace classicism" entails a "staunch conception of classic textuality against which progressive practice relies for its very definition".[6] Instead, Klinger posits that the differences to classical form that the progressive or counter-cinema text displays might be seen not as partisan components of a "subversive text", but rather as essential functioning elements of a system that thrives on a play of variation and regulation. In other words, the "disruptions" that Comolli and Narboni saw as indications of ideological contradictions in classic Hollywood films, were, on the contrary, "the modifications necessary to the maintenance and persistence" of the Hollywood system, rather than attempts to dismantle the system from within. "Critical assumptions which so measure the subversiveness of a film, based on its anti-classical formal attributes," writes Klinger, "underestimate the means through which supervising systems negotiate a normative function for even the most excessive, foregrounded, deformative textual tendencies."[7]

In delineating the typical characteristics of the Hollywood progressive text, Klinger cites the 1970s horror film, the film noir, the woman's film, the 1950s melodrama, and the exploitation B-picture as types of films usually accorded a "radical valence" by post-Comolli and Narboni critics, indicating that, by 1984, certain film genres/periods were (and still continue to be) championed over others in this respect. As Klinger remarks, these traits display in schematic form the consistent means though which the "progressive" is critically constructed.

Thus, a pessimistic world view is central to the progressive Hollywood text, in direct contrast to the optimism that characterises the "typically celebratory" view of the American way of life in classical texts. The overall atmosphere is bleak, cynical, apocalyptic and/or highly ironic. Associated with this world view are themes which dramatise, as Klinger puts it, the "demolition of dominant values" – including, the inviolability of the law and the family as an institution of social and sexual salvation (especially for women). "The center of hope in most narrative", writes Klinger, "the romantic couple, is shown as either cloyingly insipid or deranged", exploding the myth of the happy, unproblematic founding unit of the family.[8]

The overall narrative structure of the Hollywood progressive text is refined towards an exposure, rather than (as in the classical text) a suppression of ideological contradictions and tensions. Parallels are created between good and evil creating ambiguity and precluding easy identification and segregation of moral systems. And while classical texts promote the invisibility of the cause-and-effect mechanisms at work within the narrative, the progressive film departs from the classical system by either paring it down to its barest essentials so that the acknowledgement of that system is at its most minimised (for example, the exploitation film) or by exaggerating its principles to the point of stretching credibility and legibility.[9]

As Klinger points out, the issue of narrative closure is crucial. "The progressive film must escape the compromising forces inherent in the conventional procedure of closure." Whereas closure usually signals the ultimate containment of matters brought out in the narrative, progressive films end in such a way as to refuse containment of the "excessive" narrative problems produced in the course of the film: The network of cause-and-effect remains unresolved, and the narrative is not returned to a final state of equilibrium. In film noir and the 1970s horror film, as Klinger notes, narrative resolutions cannot recuperate their subversive significance, or provide redemption: "[T]he amount of violence and destructiveness centered upon the social institutions is not adequately resolved through the conventional device of closure." Instead, the usual process is circumvented through the use of certain textual strategies which undercut the affirmative ending: the "generic happy ending" brings with it a sense not of victory but of desolation, "the veneer of optimism not only unconvincing" but countered by unmistakable irony.[10]

As Klinger concludes, the cinema/ideology problematic cannot ultimately rely solely upon textual readings alone. "Industrial practices of exhibition and distribution, including promotional advertising" – extrinsic factors that are often expunged from the serious textual analysis – need to be incorporated into such readings, representing as they do the text "in practice", an "intersection at which multiple and 'extra-textual' practices of signification circulate". Furthermore, "the proliferation of diverse and co-existing representations at any given conjuncture", Klinger writes, "would suggest the pliability, rather than the rigidity of ideology". In other words, ideology allows for variety and for regulated forms of excess in the interests of its own continuity. The progressive Hollywood text may in fact be part of the "economy of variation, rather than rupture".[11]

If we were to apply Klinger's conclusions to *Dawn of the Dead*, it may be possible to claim its excesses as being part of "the economy of variation, rather than rupture": in other words, Romero's film operates as a commodity itself within the very commodity culture it critiques.[12] However, it would also be true to say that in 1978 *Dawn* posed *significant* challenges to Hollywood's distribution and regulation practices, particularly in terms of its length and its graphic violence. It was, to put it simply, too long and too strong for many in the industry to take. As critic A. Loudermilk has said, Romero refused to conform to the norms of commodification to the extent that *Dawn* might be regarded as a sort of "anti-commodity".[13] In his attempt to subvert commercial norms, Romero was innovative as he was disruptive.

Dawn of the Dead's Excessive Running Time

Although Romero had originally estimated the first cut of *Dawn* to run about two hours (based on timings of the working draft script), the improvisation added during the second part of the shoot swelled the initial assembly of edited footage to a reported 174 minutes (some sources claim that early cast and crew screenings of the first assembled version ran between 210 and 240 minutes). It is not unusual for the rough cut of a film to run far longer than its finalised version, and Romero gradually tightened the movie, according to Rubinstein, "based on audience reactions at test screenings".[14] However, he was reluctant to reduce the final running time to less than 120 minutes. This proved to be the first obstacle in finding a US distributor: the running time caused concerns for sales agents, who thought it too long for an exploitation movie, as it was perceived. Here *Dawn* would set a precedent. Although such horror films as *The Exorcist* and *Rosemary's Baby* (1968) had clocked in at longer than two hours (122 minutes and 137 minutes respectively), these had been prestigious studio productions with guaranteed distribution, not independently-produced low budget exploitation movies. The industry wisdom of the time was that such a movie should not much exceed 90 minutes (to cut down on the costs of shipping prints, enable double-billings, etc.), and Romero's refusal to cut *Dawn* down to that length caused some distributors to walk away immediately. As Romero later explained to John Hanners and Harry Kloman:

> Running time is what they're worried about, because the industry can't handle a long running time anymore. I disagree with that; in fact, I waved flags for more running time on films. I think the biggest single problem with most of the films that are out there is that they're too short.[15]

Here, Romero was challenging distribution practices of the time which centred on the "spill and fill" factor: the need to get audiences in and out of the cinema in under two hours in order to maximise the number of film screenings per day.

> They sell more candy that way, they run more shows and they don't have to keep the theatre open longer. But it's a crock, because they will keep the theater open longer for a midnight show if the film is successful. So I don't think it's meaningful. I think they are kidding themselves.[16]

For Romero, the result of these distribution practices meant that filmmakers did not have time to do what they wanted to do: "[Y]ou can't, in ninety minutes, tell an intelligent story and be spectacular with the effects."[17] This, for Romero, impacted on how effectively the film came across to audiences and, consequently, the audience's enjoyment and appreciation of the film. It is important to note that Romero's holding out for *Dawn*'s lengthy running time in the domestic market was based, at least partly, on favourable preview screenings of the 139-minute cut that he had prepared for the Cannes Film Market in May 1978 and the film's success abroad prior to its eventual US release. It is also true that he had suffered cuts to his films in the past which he felt had had a detrimental effect on their box office. The distributor, Cambist, insisted that Romero take 15 minutes out of *The Crazies* prior to release in 1973, resulting in a film that Romero felt was "too frantic".[18] And while he recognised that *Martin*'s running time of 96 minutes (reduced from 150 minutes) was necessary commercially, Romero also lamented the loss of background detail and mood in making those cuts. Neither film had fared well in the marketplace. As Romero wrote in 1987: "I still believe that most films should be longer... would be better if they were longer. Often a film that seems too long is, in fact, too short. With more character description and more sub-plotting boredom is lessened."[19]

Martin Scorsese once said of James Stewart's character in *Vertigo* (1958) that by the end of the movie it feels as if we have experienced an entire lifetime with him. That degree of empathy with a protagonist in a horror film is rare – again we think of Mia Farrow's character in *Rosemary's Baby* – and length is arguably a factor. We need time to spend with the character; to experience fully their character arc, usually over three acts, as we would a character in a stage play. *Dawn of the Dead*, as a relatively long film, does allow us to do that. What's more, we come to identify not just with an individual but with the group, and with their sense of cooperative social endeavour as they take refuge in the mall. We come to understand their individual "journeys" within that. It is probably true to say that this element – crucial to Romero's narrative design (his "pedantic kind of structure") – would have been lost if Romero had succumbed to pressure to cut the film down to commercial exploitation movie length. Romero continued his campaign of longer, more languid filmmaking with *Knightriders* and *Creepshow* (1982), both of which clock in at over 120 minutes. However, he shifted gears with the release version of *Day* of the Dead, which was, in his words "the tightest, most linear, most coherent that I've written".[20] Romero's more recent Dead movies, with their tightly-plotted action and brisk running times, have followed suit. However, it is perhaps significant that Dawn is the film most beloved by Romero's fans, and its satisfyingly lengthy narrative is arguably one of the reasons for that.

This aspect of Dawn's excess, then, was carefully thought through by Romero during the editing process. However, one of the consequences of producing a film of such length was the proliferation of different versions prepared by distributors for various international territories. The first public screening of Dawn took place in May 1978 at Cannes: the 139-minute version of the film that has subsequently been released on DVD. At Cannes, Dawn sold to Neue Constantin Film in Germany, Nippon Herald Films in Japan, and United Artists for release in South America and Australia. These and other distributors released modified versions of Dario Argento's European cut of the film – which differs significantly to both Romero's "Cannes Cut" and his final US theatrical release version. A recent inventory by scholar Charles F. Gray lists no less than nineteen different cuts of Dawn of the Dead (three of which are fan-edits) running from 95 minutes ("The Japanese Broadcast TV Cut") to 155 minutes ("The Ultimate Final Cut" by Germany's Astro DVD).[21] Censorship, of course, is a factor in different territories creating their own versions. However, many of these versions contain scenes which Romero himself ultimately left on the cutting room floor: an intriguing aspect of Dawn's excess in relation to its running time. Romero, for his part, finalised his own 126-minute theatrical cut in April, 1979. It is this version that he called his "preferred" version.

WARNER BROTHERS AND AIP

The difficulty Romero and Rubinstein had in finding a US distributor for Dawn resulted not just from the film's length, but also from its graphic violence. Eventually Romero and Rubinstein went with United Film Distribution Company, a subsidiary of United Artists Theatre Circuit (a movie theatre chain owned by United Artists Communications), who agreed to put Dawn out uncut and unrated. According to Rubinstein, "none of the major companies would agree to that".[22] A case can be made, then, for Dawn as an outlier film on this basis. It is not that Rubinstein could not find a major distributor for the film, but that he and Romero *declined* distribution with a major as they were not willing to cut the film in line with industry and censorship requirements.

Several major distributors had, in fact, been interested. The first had been United Artists themselves, who, as previously mentioned, acquired *Dawn* for South America and Australia. However, according to Christopher Koetting, they refused to distribute the film in the US due to its violent content.[23] United Artists have a long history of working with independent filmmakers, in the words of Tino Balio, "granting filmmakers autonomy and creative freedom over the making of their pictures and by rewarding talent with a share of the profits".[24] This they had been doing since the 1950s, at a time when the majors were still operating the studio system of production whereby creative control was vested in the studio chief. UA had also recently taken risks with controversial and censorable subject matter such as *The Last Tango in Paris* (1973). It is likely that they did not want to be associated with an exploitation film in the domestic market, which is probably why they declined *Dawn* for the US but, as Koetting remarks, "had no such compunction about releasing it in South America and Australia".[25] UA possibly also foresaw the problems that *Dawn* would have with the MPAA domestically, and did not want to handle an unrated release or a film with an 'X' certificate. (UA did, in fact, finance, along with UFD, Romero's next film, *Knightriders*.)

Warner Brothers and American International Pictures expressed a serious interest in the film. Both would perhaps have been a good 'fit'. Warners had handled controversial films in the early 1970s – *A Clockwork Orange*, *The Devils* (1971) – with great success. *The Exorcist* had, of course, generated huge box office based on controversy. As well, the company had acquired Larry Cohen's independent movie *It's Alive*, which had turned out to be a surprise hit when Warners reissued it in 1977. AIP had, of course, built its reputation on independent low budget exploitation since the 1950s, and in the 1970s was seen as one of the most stable companies in Hollywood. By 1978, though, AIP was moving more into the mainstream, with such titles as *Force 10 from Navarone* (1978), *Meteor* (1979) and *Love at First Bite* (1979). As Romero later remarked of these distributors, "people rode [*Dawn*] like a pony, but would always come out of the screening room and say 'that's really rough. What can we do to clean this up a little bit'. But Richard and I both believed that the film's best chance of success was to let it be as strong as possible."[26]

Both Warners and AIP made Romero and Rubinstein offers for the US distribution, but under the stipulation that they cut the film in order to get an "R" rating from the MPAA. Romero and Rubinstein knew that this would, in effect, eviscerate the film, and held out for an unrated release. However, as Gagne comments, Warners didn't have the capacity, as a blanket corporate policy, to release an unrated movie; and AIP felt that an unrated picture was not befitting of their drive toward respectability.[27]

Rubinstein and Romero's decision to turn down Warner Brothers and AIP is an interesting gamble that ultimately paid off. It came at a time when financially it would have been easier for them to accept either deal – the budget for *Dawn* had been spent (indeed, Rubinstein had been forced to seek additional private investment to pay for the film's postproduction costs) and, according to Gagne, "there was barely enough left in Laurel's bank account to pay the rent at the end of each month".[28] However, for Rubinstein, holding out for a distributor who was willing to release the film unrated made good business sense, as he explained in 1987:

> You really make money in this business not in the first week, but where a picture has played for a substantial period of time and people keep coming even though you've stopped advertising. I didn't feel that cutting the film would promote that kind of situation – there's a difference between getting wide distribution and making money. We felt that *Dawn* was strong enough to make up for the business problems of going without a rating by doing well at the box office. It wasn't that I didn't recognise those problems; I just assigned a dollar value to them, and then I said to myself "Well, do I expect this movie to cover those costs?" And I did.[29]

THE ARGENTO CUT

Rubinstein's optimism for an unrated US release was boosted by *Dawn*'s box office opening in Italy, (under the title *Zombi*) in September, 1978, where it topped the chart in Rome, Milan, Turin and Florence, against competition from the likes of *Coma* (1978), *Saturday Night Fever* (1978) and *The Swarm* (1978). Partly, its number one success in these key cities was due to a dearth of Italian product that season, with Argento's name helping to draw in Italian audiences. *Dawn* would gross $1 million in its first six weeks in Italy. Interest in *Dawn* had been generated in Italian cinemas in the summer of 1978 by a very graphic trailer (based on the Argento cut of the film) that revealed some of the film's extreme gore, including disembowelling, beheading and the gruesome biting of neck and arm. Argento's name is prominent in the trailer credits, with his business partners, Claudio Argento and Alfredo Cuomo, rather than Rubinstein, billed as the film's producers (Rubinstein is credited as Executive Producer).

Although Romero recognised that the business deal he had with Argento on *Dawn* was a good one, with Laurel retaining the English-speaking rights (which represented the lion's share of the market), there are indications that he was less than happy with Argento's version of the film. Argento had, according to Peter Schöfböck, removed many of the quieter character development scenes (as well as replacing much of the DeWolfe library soundtrack with Goblin), resulting in "an overall darker, faster-paced and more 'serious' film that quite deliberately has filtered out any satirical or even comical elements to become a straightforward horror-action shocker".[30] Argento's reason for doing this, according to Romero, was that "he felt that some of the jokes and humor would not be recognisable to a foreign audience".[31] There is the sense, however, that Argento had ultimately downgraded Romero's film to exploitation for the youth market. Although he remained diplomatic about Argento's treatment of the film, comments that Romero made over the years suggested that he was not happy with the result. "What he took out was essentially what I'll call the subtleties, the valleys,"[32] Romero told Gagne in 1987. Indeed, Romero may have blamed some of the censorship problems that *Dawn* encountered in European territories, such as Germany, on the exploitative nature of Argento's version, which (in Rubinstein's words) lacked "a rationale for the violence".[33]

Romero was not happy with Argento's approach to the soundtrack either, as he told *Starburst* in 1982: "The Italian (version) missed more things out than had in. I don't mean the violent aspects, but the humour and characterisation. The music is also wall-to-wall Goblin whereas I wanted to make use of the shopping mall muzak and use the Goblin for the more traditional scoring elements."[34] Romero recognised that Argento's brand of cinematic "excess" differed to his own, and was one geared towards intensity. As Rubinstein has observed: "Dario's style is even more directly intense than George's. George can take you up to a hundred miles an hour through most of the picture, but

George A. Romero editing Dawn of the Dead.

there are valleys, quiet moments. Dario has a tendency never to leave a quiet moment and go hell-bent all the way through."[35] Romero had in fact tried to integrate the two styles in his 126-minute version, which he finalised after Argento's cut had been released. But he was not able to do so to the extent that he would have liked. Much of this attempt at integration was though the use of Goblin tracks. As Romero told Tony Williams:

> It was unfortunate that I didn't really have a lot of chances to integrate those Goblin tracks. I used a lot of very traditional songs and funky stuff like the Muzak. Goblin were doing one third track simultaneously and the tracks on our version are a little bit harder because I like a lot of their music. Dario's version on his European score has a lot more Goblin. But he went the other way. He tried to do that *Suspiria* experience. But we didn't really have the film to fit into that. Neither version is exactly what it should be. But I was trying to bring it close so I used some other kind of library music that bridged between Goblin and the other traditional stuff.[36]

UFD

Romero's dissatisfaction with the Argento cut may have made him even more determined not to trim *Dawn* down for distributors, or to make drastic cuts in order to achieve an "R". Relinquishing final cut in Europe no doubt strengthened his resolve not to give up control of his film in the US. This was at a time when the MPAA's chairman Richard Heffner had personally informed Rubinstein that "there isn't a list of cuts long enough" for *Dawn* to avoid an "X".[37]

To prove to UFD that there was an audience for *Dawn*, Rubinstein resorted to the independent film practice of "four-walling" the movie in New York. That is, where filmmakers or distributors hire a cinema to show their film to the general public, retaining any ticket sales and opportunity to secure a review in a major newspaper. The downside of four-walling is that a film can become tainted as inadequate for ordinary programming by a theatre or acquisition by a distributor. Given *Dawn*'s box office success in Italy, Rubinstein's decision to four-wall *Dawn* is all the more remarkable as a challenge to conventional industry wisdom. UFD had expressed a serious interest in the American rights to *Dawn* since a screening of the film at the international media market, MIFED, in October, 1978. But, like Warners and AIP, they had reservations about releasing the film unrated. Rubinstein's New York preview was an attempt to overcome those reservations by showing that *Dawn* had box office potential in the US as it had in Italy. *The Pittsburgh Post-Gazette* (8 December, 1978) reported the preview as taking place the previous weekend: "The theatre sold out and several hundred fans were turned away."[38] The audience's wild response to the film finally convinced UFD that they were onto a winner, and a deal was quickly struck with Rubinstein and Romero to release the film unrated.

It is important to note that UFD, whilst a small subsidiary of the United Artists Theatre Circuit, was not per se a grindhouse distributor, or a maverick outfit like Bryanston (whose films include *Andy Warhol's Frankenstein* [1973], *The Texas Chain Saw Massacre* and *Dark Star* [1974]). It did, however, generally handle titles that UATC didn't considered appropriate for its nationwide chain of first-run theatres. Prior to *Dawn*, UFD had distributed West German sex comedy *Das sündige Bett* (*A Single Bed*, 1973), René Cardona's 1977 exploitative *Jaws* rip-off *Tintorera* and sleeper hit *The Kentucky Fried Movie* (1977). These were films that were not thought to have the box office potential of a studio release. Here, *Dawn* differed somewhat, as it had already been a hit in Italy. Traditionally, films released without a rating in the US are usually small independents, foreign films or other types of movies not expected to receive wide distribution. Here again, *Dawn* would differ from the industry norm. Laurel announced to the press on February 1, 1979 that UFD would be opening *Dawn* in key cities in April 1979, with a 500-theatre saturation release planned for July in UATC houses.[39] In practice, UFD were following a tried and tested distribution pattern of a roadshow theatrical release in which a film opens at a few cinemas in key cities before circulating among cinemas around the country. However, the grosses were considerable from the start. *Dawn* earned several times its advertising budget in the first week of its New York engagement, and the box office take dropped only 10% in its second week, "a sign of extraordinary legs", as Rubinstein remarked in 1987.[40] By May 2, *Dawn* was ranked at number 4 in the national US box office chart.

There is no doubt that Laurel's relationship with UFD was beneficial to Romero — at least at the start. Laurel entered into a three-picture financing and distribution deal with UFD in 1978, which gave some financial stability to Romero, enabling him to make *Knightriders*, *Creepshow* and *Day of the Dead*. However, the limitations of budget and distribution in working with a small company like UFD (and therefore the financial returns to Laurel) at the same time spurred Romero and Rubinstein to seek relationships with the Hollywood majors. As Romero remarked to Tom Seligson in 1981, "I'm the first one on the plane whenever (the studios) want to talk. I have not resisted them in any way, shape or form. I know people at all the major studios, and I'm always in conversation with them."[41] A surprising remark, perhaps, from a filmmaker who has always had the reputation of a maverick, but also an insight into the realities of independent film production and distribution in the 1980s when it was becoming increasingly difficult for companies like Laurel to make money back on their movies. (When Laurel released its annual financial report for the fiscal year ending March 31, 1981, it recorded a net loss of $237,663.)[42]

On UFD's part, *Dawn* was handled in such a way that maximised its profit potential as the touted "biggest cult blockbuster of all time". As well as expanding its national theatrical engagements, UFD entered it into the drive-in circuit and nurtured it as a midnight movie. It is noticeable, though, how *Dawn* was treated increasingly like low budget exploitation theatrically. In upstate New York drive-ins as early as summer 1979 it was being paired in double-bills with musty old movies like *Whatever Happened to*

Aunt Alice? (1969) or low grade sleaze like *Meatcleaver Massacre* (1977). This type of theatrical double feature billing continued into the 1980s when UFD released *Dawn* in May 1981 with Troma's *Mother's Day* (1980). Finally, UFD took the step of cutting *Dawn* to gain an "R", so that it could play in a double-billing with *Creepshow* in May 1983. More than 50 cuts were needed to satisfy the MPAA, rendering *Dawn* almost incomprehensible. As one fan, who sat through the "R"-rated version, recalled, "instead of opening *Dawn* to a wider audience, it simply alienated itself".[43] The resulting uproar from audiences and fans was such that UFD quickly withdrew this version from release, and issued a statement to the press:

> Due to radical rejection from the long-time cult followers of *Dawn of the Dead*,
> United Film Distribution has taken the position of surrendering the R rating certificate
> to the MPAA, and will in future release *Dawn of the Dead* in its original state, as an
> unrated picture.[44]

"Rebel text" or no, it seems audiences, at least, wanted *Dawn of the Dead* in its full extremity.

FOOTNOTES

1. Wood, *Hollywood from Vietnam to Reagan*, 287
2. Jean-Louis Comolli and Jean Narboni, "Cinema/Ideology/Criticism", in Bill Nichols (ed.) *Movies and Methods: Vol 1*, (Berkeley: University of California Press, 1976), 24.
3. Ibid., 25.
4. Ibid., 27.
5. Robin Wood, "Ideology, Genre, Auteur", in Barry Keith Grant (ed.) *Film Reader II*, (Austin: University of Texas Press, 1995), 63.
6. Barbara Klinger, "'Cinema/Ideology/Criticism'" Revisited: The Progressive Text", in *Screen*, 25 (1), 1984, 33.
7. Ibid., 42-43.
8. Ibid., 35-36.
9. Ibid., 37.
10. Ibid.
11. Ibid., 44.
12. This becomes particularly intriguing when considering Romero's early career making advertisements/commercials in the Image Ten and Laurel periods, and the ways in which

he then recasts these skills towards consumer critique in the *Dawn*'s satire (perhaps most apparent in the consumerism montage upon the quartet's settling into the mall).

13. A. Loudermilk. "Eating 'Dawn' in the Dark: Zombie desire and commodified identity in George A. Romero's 'Dawn of the Dead'", 83.
14. George Anderson, "The Triangle Tattler", *The Pittsburgh Post-Gazette*, February 5, 1979, 16.
15. Hanners and Kloman, "The McDonaldization of America: An Interview with George A. Romero", 90.
16. Ibid.
17. Ibid.
18. Gagne, *The Zombies That Ate Pittsburgh: The Films of George A. Romero*, 56.
19. Ibid., 81.
20. Ibid., 170.
21. Source https://www.facebook.com/groups/officialnightofthelivingdead/ permalink/1673732526108518
22. Crawley, "Richard P. Rubinstein on Romero", *Starburst*, no. 46, 39.
23. Koetting, "No More Room in Hell", *The Dark Side*, 19.
24. Tino Balio, United Artists: The Company that Changed the Film Industry, (Madison: University of Wisconsin Press, 1987), 3.
25. Koetting, "No More Room in Hell", *The Dark Side*, 19.
26. Martin, *The Dead Will Walk*.
27. Gagne, *The Zombies That Ate Pittsburgh: The Films of George A. Romero*, 98.
28. Ibid., 99.
29. Ibid., 98.
30. Source: Peter Schöfböck, "History", WGON, http://www.dawnofthedead.co.uk/history/
31. Gagne, *The Zombies That Ate Pittsburgh: The Films of George A. Romero*, 98.
32. Ibid.
33. Ibid.
34. Jones, "George Romero", *Starburst*, 36.
35. Gagne, *The Zombies That Ate Pittsburgh: The Films of George A. Romero*, 84.
36. Lippe, Williams, and Wood, "The George Romero Interview, Toronto Film Festival, September 15th, 1979". *Cinema Spectrum*, 68.
37. Source: Peter Schöfböck, "History", *WGON*, http://www.dawnofthedead.co.uk/history/
38. *The Pittsburgh Post-Gazette*, December 8, 1978, 23.
39. *The Pittsburgh Post-Gazette*, February 5, 1979, 16.
40. Gagne, *The Zombies That Ate Pittsburgh: The Films of George A. Romero*, 100.
41. Seligson, "George Romero: Revealing the Monsters Within Us", *Rod Serling's Twilight Zone Magazine*, 86.
42. Jennifer Lin, "Low Budget Laurel Sees Profit in Horror", *The Pittsburgh Post-Gazette*, August 27,

1981, 12.

43. Source: "Versions", *The Zombie Farm*, http://www2.gol.com/users/noman/?fbclid=IwAR2geNUt
nYifLYsq6w2HDP5Phqln2umZLH0qCGHq-BMzxqZ8_-IPPFp3CiQ

44. Source: Peter Schöfböck, "History", *WGON*, http://www.dawnofthedead.co.uk/history/

CHAPTER 5: "SICK OR SUBTLE?": CRITICAL RECEPTION AND AUDIENCE CONSUMPTION

"By blitzing *Jaws* territory," wrote critic Tom Allen in *The Village Voice* (April 30, 1979), "this truly independent movie will pose the challenge of the decade to the way films are made, rated, and marketed in America. I think it's going to be the biggest cult blockbuster of all time."[1] Indeed, the excesses of *Dawn of the Dead* would not only challenge the film industry but critics and audiences, too. It is perhaps to be expected that a film as excessive as *Dawn* would provoke equally extreme reactions in the press and from the viewing public. The critical reaction initially dismayed Romero, who felt that the film was not being judged on its own merits. Prominent critics, such as Janet Maslin of the *New York Times*, boasted of walking out of the film after fifteen minutes, disgusted by its gore. C.W. Smith of *The Dallas Times-Herald*, proclaimed it "the most horrific, brutal, nightmarish descent into hell (literally) ever put on screen, and its power can be gauged by the peals of maniacal laughter bursting forth from many of us who survived the movie's first few moments. The film gave me nightmares so severe that I awoke afraid to return to sleep, its frames burned forever on my consciousness in an indelible way."[2] Very few critics managed to give it a balanced, unemotional review on its first release.

Much of the polarisation of critical opinion arose from the graphic (and taboo-breaking) on-screen violence, which, for its time, was unsurpassed (indeed, it is easy to forget, over forty years – and numerous gore movies – later, how shocking *Dawn* was at the time in terms of its "splatter"). A number of early criticisms concentrated on the violence, and the effect this appeared to have on some members of the audience. These criticisms keyed into media effects debates and, in particular, concerns about the desensitisation of viewers to screen violence that seemed to preoccupy the censors. In many cases, these concerns preoccupied *Dawn*'s early reviewers, too. The film itself came second to a broader discussion of screen violence – or was dismissed altogether because of its violence. As Romero complained at the time, "I don't care if the *New York Times* doesn't like the film, but at least they should write a real review of it".[3] In the case of *Dawn*, the media effects debate has receded over the years and critics now tend to focus on the satirical aspects of the film. The gore of *Dawn of the Dead* has become commonplace to the genre; its shock/controversy factor has been lost, which has led to the film becoming less polarising for critics and audiences. In fact, *Dawn* is now almost universally praised as "one of the most compelling and entertaining zombie films ever" (*Rotten Tomatoes*): "*Dawn of the Dead* perfectly blends pure horror and gore with social commentary on material society."[4] But the violent extremity of *Dawn* has, in the past, been seen by many as problematic, just as its gory excess has contributed to its cult status amongst audiences.

CRITICAL RECEPTION

Dawn received its United States premiere in Pittsburgh at the Gateway Theatre on 12 April, 1979. In lieu of an MPAA rating, UFD took the step of adding a warning to *Dawn*'s advertising and poster art: "There is no explicit sex in this picture. However, there are scenes of violence which may be considered shocking. No-one under 17 will be admitted." Rubinstein maintains that the self-imposed adult restriction was used responsibly and not as a marketing technique. However, it seems that even in the premiere there were members of the audience under 17, and young teenagers would attend the film across the States on its first release. There were complaints of cinemas not adhering to the self-imposed age restriction and this no doubt fuelled the controversy amongst critics opposed to the film's violence and hostile to unrated movies generally – just as had happened with *Night of the Living Dead* a decade earlier.

The *Pittsburgh Press* review of the premiere indicates how even local reviewers were dismayed by the film's effect on the youth audience, and how this complicated their own responses to *Dawn*. Reviewer Ed Blank starts his April 13, 1979 review by calling *Dawn* "the most gruesome film to open" in Pittsburgh.[5] He acknowledges UFD's self-imposed age restriction but expresses concern that "even 17 may be too young". This he bases on the "appalling reaction of some members of the college age audience" whom he calls "too immature to handle the moral ramifications". Interestingly, Blank's own response to the film's violence is to recognise the "moral ramifications" that Romero intended the film to raise:

The human characters, by looting and enjoying violence so much, forfeit some of the empathy that otherwise would be theirs. They also push *Dawn* beyond the routine perimeter of horror films – past the 'nightmare' conflict of human and 'non-human' – into a sphere in which humanly evil people take on the helplessly once-human… Most of the humans might as well be zombies, the film says implicitly, they're destroying each other mindlessly anyway.[6]

Yet for Blank this complexity was lost on the audience, whose reaction he found more disturbing than the movie itself. "Clearly, *Dawn* was appreciated," he writes. "There was plenty of positive reaction: rooting, laughing and gasping. One can, with reservations, understand the glee with which some of the gruesome action is watched; it's visceral and gaudy." What concerns Blank, though, is when the audience "cheer looting and applaud anti-heroic violence", which for him, creates "horror more real than any in the movie".

Blank ends his review there, with no discussion of why the audience may have responded this way to these elements in the film. Instead, there is the implication that *Dawn* might encourage anti-social behaviour in the audience, particularly in younger viewers. Admittedly, even Romero himself would profess to being worried by the reactions of some audiences to the scenes of looting, prompting him to comment "nobody is going to come out of *Dawn of the Dead* and eat someone",[7] whilst conceding that "it might just cause somebody to try to break into a shopping mall".[8] For Richard Lippe, the audience's reaction suggests a sense of catharsis or exhilaration at seeing "a shopping mall smashed up" instead of the "dangerous fantasy of having possession of the mall".[9] It follows that *Dawn*'s effect on audiences might be to vent anti-social impulses rather than encourage anti-social behaviour. There is, moreover, an assumed cultural superiority implicit in Blank's commentary: that he is able to appreciate the film's "moral ramifications" whereas the general public is not.

Two local readers of the *Pittsburgh Press* who had attended the Gala premiere of *Dawn* picked Blank up on this in letters sent to the newspaper. "I do not pretend to be a movie critic," wrote Nancy J. Hanzel of Swissvale, 'but while he was looking for moral ramifications he overlooked the simplicity of the story line, that being man's attempt to survive in a world gone awry." Hanzel, as have many other fans of the film, enjoyed

Dawn primarily as a survivalist horror narrative. "I never got the impression the violence and looting were for fun," she states. "They were the necessities of life." For her the special effects were "magnificent" and clearly part of the film's fantasy element. However, she notes that the under 17 restriction was not enforced, and claims that there were children as young as 7 or 8 years old in the audience "who should not have been there".[10] Similar concerns had been raised about *Night of the Living Dead* when it was released in 1968, before the introduction of the MPAA ratings system. By the late 1960s, due largely to the TV success of *The Munsters* and reruns of old horror films on TV, horror movies were marketed primarily to children; matinee screenings of horror films were often attended by audiences of kids. The critic Roger Ebert attended one such matinee at the Adams Theatre in Newark, New Jersey in 1969 where *Night* happened to be playing on a double-bill with *Dr Who and the Daleks* (1965). Ebert wrote in the *Chicago Sun-Times*:

> I don't think the younger kids knew what hit them. This was ghouls eating people up – and you could see actually see what they were eating. This was little girls killing their mothers. I felt real terror in that neighbourhood theatre. I saw kids who had no resources they could draw upon to protect themselves from the dread and fear they felt. I suppose the idea was to make a fast buck. But I don't know how I could explain it to kids who left the theatre with tears in their eyes.[11]

Although Ebert would later revise his negative review of *Night* in light of its subsequent critical reappraisal, his attack on *Night* caused Romero a good deal of bad publicity. (Ebert's main target was actually not the film at all but the lack of a ratings system to protect children from inappropriate movies; Ebert's review was part of a campaign that eventually led to the MPAA introducing an age rating in cinemas – but *Night* was a handy scapegoat in that campaign.)

The concerns expressed by critics and the viewing public to young audiences attending *Night* and *Dawn* related directly to the extremity of these films. In the opinion of the critics, these were not creaky old horror movies but "ghouls eating people up" in graphic detail – and therefore unsuitable for children. Even so, a number of young viewers have expressed their appreciation of *Dawn*, with some fans claiming to have first seen it as young as five years old. The second letter sent to the *Pittsburgh Press* was, in fact, from a young attendee of the Gala premiere, who was incensed by Blank's suggestion that the age limit for the movie should be raised higher. "Although I am only 14 years old, I went to the film anyway and even Mr. Blank could find nothing wrong with my actions at the movie," wrote Stan Berman of Baldwin. "I know many others who could go to the movie without incurring any complaints. The right to see a movie shouldn't be denied to the young just because some abuse it." Berman's indignation is clear from the opening line of his letter in which he states: "It's time people realized that age isn't the only thing that controls maturity."[12]

As well as the extreme violence of *Dawn*, local critics objected to the film's length and the "simplicity" of the storyline. "Too long, simple, boring," opined *Pittsburgh Post-Gazette* critic Donald Miller in his April 14, 1979 review. Although acknowledging Romero's desire to have the film taken as a comic book, Miller claims that *Dawn* is overstated is this respect. "The movie is so violent," writes Miller, "that the viewer moves from revulsion to boredom fairly soon." Miller does not recognise the moral ramifications indicated by Blank, but admits that "the picture is frightening, both from standard surprise shots and the excessive killing". For Miller the length of the film contributes to it being "too repetitious to sustain much interest". Indeed Miller, alongside a number of critics of the time, seems reluctant to read *Dawn* on any level other than cheap exploitation. "Its violence is its claim to fame," he concludes. "The real point to this picture seems to be to see how far its makers went to make a low-grade horror flick horrible."[13] This cultural animosity towards the horror genre – particularly films operating in the E.C. tradition of subversive graphic content – would colour the reviewers of a number of national critics, too. Gary Arnold of *The Washington Post* dismissed Romero's ironies as not "subtle or devastating enough to justify lengthy contemplation", whilst again relegating the film to status of exploitation: "*Dawn* seems like a good 80-minute horror premise stretched out at half an hour too long."[14]

Despite the reservations of some local critics and members of the public, *Dawn* clicked with audiences immediately in its home town (which had not been the case with Romero's previous films). On 24 April, 1979, the *Pittsburgh Post-Gazette* reported that *Dawn* was doing "phenomenal business", with the first week grosses at three Pittsburgh theatres estimated at $55,000.[15] The film's early success in the States and in Italy may also have influenced national reviewers, polarising opinion more than might otherwise have been the case had audiences not flocked to *Dawn*. In other words, the popular success of *Dawn* may have made the film somewhat more distasteful for some reviewers.

The New York critics, in particular, split into two distinct camps of lovers and haters. Of the latter, most famous is Maslin's walk-out during the film's press screening. This followed a number of similar walk-outs at the 1979 Dallas Film Festival by conservative viewers who objected to the film being "schlock disguised as art". Maslin's reason for leaving, as stated in her review of April 20, 1979 was her "pet peeve about flesh-eating zombies that never stop snacking".[16] After receiving a number of complaints from the public, she would regret walking out of the film and reviewing it anyway, telling Aaron Arradillas in 2019, "I hated it and thought I was being funny, but I took a lot of heat – justifiably – for walking out… If I had known how influential the *Times* critic was at the time of *Dawn of the Dead*, I wouldn't have left."[17] Her editor, Vincent Canby, supported Maslin's non-review despite public criticism, and his doubling down on the film involved a total dismissal of it – and of its audience: "Fake mayhem and not worth getting exercised about. If simulated cannibalism is your dish, then go and enjoy it. If not, stay away."[18] Canby's antipathy to the film was no surprise to Romero: the critic had similarly dismissed *Night* with a three-sentence review in 1968, describing it as "a grainy little movie acted by what appear to be non-professional actors, who are besieged in a farmhouse by some other non-professional actors, who stagger around stiff-legged pretending to be flesh-eating ghouls".[19] However, Romero was right to publicly call the *New York Times* out for not writing a proper review of *Dawn*.

Robin Wood has decried the "bourgeois elitism" of such critics, attacking their inability or unwillingness to give serious attention to films that do not carry "a set of external signifiers that advertise the film as a Work of Art". This he sees as a fundamental betrayal of the relationship between critic and reader: the critic feels superior to the "muck" presented by the filmmaker; and, therefore, superior to the reader by denying a serious discussion of the film. "What I mean by bourgeois elitism," wrote Wood in 1986, "could as well be illustrated from the writings of John Simon or Pauline Kael."[20] Indeed, Kael was one of *Dawn*'s detractors in 1978, although her dismissal of the movie becomes all the more intriguing when one considers how she would embrace splatter later in her career. "You're supposed to have a strong stomach to sit through this one," wrote Kael in *The New Yorker*, 'but it's so stupefyingly obvious and repetitive that you begin to laugh with relief that you're not being emotionally affected; it's just a gross-out.'[21] Interesting, then, that she would later heap praise on the equally "gross" *Re-animator* (1985) for the same reasons:

[T]he bloodier it gets, the funnier it is. It's like pop Buñuel; the jokes hit you in a subterranean comic zone that the surrealists' pranks sometimes reached, but without the surrealists' self-consciousness (and art-consciousness). This is indigenous American junkiness, like the Mel Brooks-Gene Wilder *Young Frankenstein* (1974), but looser and more low-down.[22]

But wasn't *Dawn of the Dead* "indigenous American junkiness", too? Janet Maslin would also shower *Re-animator* with praise, despite her "pet-peeve about zombies". Of course, critics operate within the cultural "moment", and this may go some way to explain the change of heart of some reviewers.

Roger Ebert, as previously mentioned, revised his original review of *Night* (after that film had become hailed as a classic in France and England), writing in 2004, "if I were to rate it today, I'd give it 3 1/2 stars".[23] Ebert would, in fact, become one of *Dawn*'s earliest champions, inviting Romero to screen the film at the Dallas Film Festival in April 1979. Despite the controversy that *Dawn* caused at the screenings, Ebert stuck his neck out for the film, and for Romero, and attempted to give a balanced view of the film's merits and excesses. "Reviewing films like *Dawn of the Dead* presents a special problem for movie critics," he wrote in his review:

The movie is indeed – and admittedly – depraved, violent, brutal, decadent and disgusting, and cheerfully graphic in its scenes of ghouls eating human flesh. I can sympathise with the *New York Times* critic [Janet Maslin] who walked out of the film after 15 minutes (the opening scenes are of almost unrelieved mayhem). And yet if she had stayed, she would have discovered that the film had more elements than its simple violence, that this film can't easily be dismissed.[24]

Ebert goes on to discuss the Dallas festival screenings, in which *Dawn* proved to be the most controversial film. "After one screening, a shouting match developed between audience members who asked, 'What kind of sick mind could make a film like this?' and others who called it the best film in the festival." Romero, who was standing in the lobby, observed "if nobody walked out, it wouldn't be the movie I wanted to make":[25] a clear reference to the Grand Guignol/E.C. tradition in which he was working. Ebert then goes on to ask the reader to see beyond the violence to the intentions of the filmmaker, commenting on Romero's film as more "subtle and tricky in its intentions than at first it appears". This observation is based on the portrayal of the zombies in the film. "It's difficult to make up our minds about the endless violence inflicted on the zombies," Ebert remarks:

> They are shotgunned, run over, hacked to bits, decapitated by helicopter blades…
> and after a while we notice that our reaction to this mayhem is curiously complex.
> On the one hand the violence isn't as disturbing as it would be against "real" human
> beings: since the victims are without intelligence or personalities (and, for that matter,
> are already dead,) their fates are less compelling. And yet, at the same time, we feel
> a sympathy for them: it is not their fault that they are zombies, and their activities are
> deliberately anti-social. It's just in their nature to eat human flesh.

"*Dawn of the Dead*: Sick or Subtle?" ran the headline of Ebert's review, and the critic himself seems undecided. "Brilliant filmmaking that inspires extreme reactions," he concludes. "Is the film a scathing social satire or a wallowing in violence and depravity? This debate alone is what makes *Dawn of the Dead* an extraordinary film – hard to take, impossible to forget."

The ambivalent depiction of extreme violence in *Dawn* preoccupied a number of serious critics, including Robin Wood, who, along with Tony Williams and Richard Lippe, took Romero to task during their interview with him at the Toronto Film Festival in September 1979. Clearly mindful of the controversy surrounding *Dawn* on its cinema release, Wood asked Romero to comment on the "seeming paradox about the statements you attempt in your films and the majority audience's wish to see violence".[26] He goes on to compare *Dawn* to Wes Craven's treatment of violence in *The Last House on the Left* and *The Hills Have Eyes*, in which, according to Wood, the violence is so disturbing, it becomes impossible to enjoy. *Dawn*'s violence, by contrast, is enjoyable to the audience. For Wood, this presents a moral problem. Tony Williams has since remarked that Wood was unfamiliar with the E.C. tradition; Romero, for his part, has consistently claimed that *Dawn* satirises its audience by making the violence so stylised and exaggerated as to be absurd black comedy. As he replied to Wood, "playing (the violence) to its absolute extreme is what softens it".[27]

Still, a number of critics detected an element of commercial cynicism in the extremity of *Dawn*'s Grand Guignol violence. In his thesis *Apocalypticism in the Contemporary Horror Film*, written in 1983, Christopher Sharrett credits Romero with gearing the "often shocking, exploitative" violence of his early work toward a critique of the industry which relied on "the most thinly-veiled sensationalism"[28] to draw an audience. However, beneath this self-reflexive veneer, Sharrett detected in Romero's films an "anarchic and nihilistic" spirit that relies on "the traditional vision of the urban apocalypse decrying all human enterprise as futile".[29] For Sharrett, "the streak of moralism that affects Romero's satire" is diluted by "the simple urge to revel in the midst of the irreversible calamity".[30] Sharrett's reading of *Dawn of the Dead* is in keeping with this thesis.

However, Sharrett would come to revise his opinion of the film in light of its sequels and the "obsolescence" of other zombie films produced since the millennium whose "value as social/political commentary is not only almost totally gone, it has been transformed by neoconservative culture into its opposite, with audiences invited to enjoy the decapitation or blasting-apart of shambling, decaying ghouls".[31] Behind Sharrett's apparent change of heart about Romero's films, including *Dawn*, is an appreciation of Romero's symbolic use of the zombie. "One essential point of Romero's films," wrote Sharrett in 2014, "is that zombies are people, removed from the living by accident and the fact of disease and death. Their monstrousness (cannibalism) is clearly associated with the norm, with accepted human behaviour under consumer capitalism."[32] Further, Sharrett credits Romero's zombie films with offering "one of the horror film's greatest critiques of Otherness". The cannibalism of the zombies in *Dawn*, Sharrett writes

> makes the points that the real targets of capitalism are other people, who are consumed by work over which they have no control. The survivalists, the nominal heroes of the film, further extend Romero's critique of the other by way of their own jealousy, rapaciousness, and fight for their domain – a fight that becomes complicated indeed when they face off a motorcycle gang, one of cinema's emblems of a reversion to barbarism.[33]

Any qualms that Sharratt may have about Romero's apocalyptic nihilism have been assuaged by the conviction that "together, Romero's first trilogy constitutes one of the most scathing cinematic critiques of America from the 1960s to the 1980s. Its project is comprehensive enough to constitute the total dismissal of American ideology."[34]

It is worth mentioning here that a number of '70s horror films prior to *Dawn of the Dead* had raised the ire of contemporary reviewers due to their extreme violence. Most notorious is *Last House on the Left*, which Roger Ebert had championed as "tough, bitter little sleeper of movie",[35] but which had suffered walk outs by other critics – notably, Howard Thompson of the *New York Times*, who claimed to have left the screening after 50 minutes, later describing the film as "sickening tripe".[36] Similarly, *The Texas Chain Saw Massacre* was described as "despicable" by a *Los Angeles Times* critic and labelled "sadistic" by a number of reviewers.[37] Both films caused public protests outside movie theatres in the United States, largely stirred up by such negative press coverage. This led to bans in a number of countries, including in Great Britain, where both films were denied certificates on first release and remained unavailable for a number of years, both theatrically and later on home video. The notoriety of these key films in the "American Nightmare" cycle would impact on *Dawn of the Dead*, leading to censorship problems for Romero's film, as discussed in the following chapter.

AUDIENCE CONSUMPTION

There seems little doubt that audiences enjoyed *Dawn*'s excesses on its first release, as they continue to do so today, but that does not explain the film's particular popularity in suburban theatres, where it grossed more at the box office than it did at urban venues, especially during its Pittsburgh and New York openings in 1979. As Romero himself remarked at the time, "It seems to do better at the suburbs everywhere, for some reason. It's doing more in New Rochelle than at the Rivoli on Broadway."[38] In Pittsburgh, attendance dropped off steeply at the Gateway in downtown Pittsburgh where the film had its premiere. However, at the Cinemette East in Monroeville, 13 miles outside of Pittsburgh, audiences continued to flock to the film. As the *Pittsburgh Post-Gazette* reported on 24 April, 1979, "customers were lined up across the lobby the other night. The film was shot just across the parking lot in the Monroeville Mall."[39] What

Dawn of the Dead *at the Rivoli on Broadway during its New York opening in 1979.*

Monroeville and New Rochelle have in common is that they might be described as "mall towns"; the siting of large indoor shopping malls, such as Monroeville Mall, took place in the suburbs, rather than cities. It follows that suburban audiences in 1979 would be more familiar with the then-relatively new phenomenon of the out-of-town shopping mall than would some urban audiences. Many urban filmgoers, in 1979, would not yet have "walked the mall".

Critic and *Dawn* fan A. Loudermilk recalls how his own first viewing coincided with his introduction to mall culture as a working-class suburban teenager:

> My small town marks the midway point between two college towns, but in 1980 most kids my age referred to these only as "mall towns". I was always jealous of kids who went "malling" regularly, and to go to both malls over the course of a single weekend was an excess to be bragged about all week… And at the time of *Dawn of the Dead*, the dawn of the '80s, the dawn of my teens, I was just coming into a real desperation to fit in, to be popular, to be standardized by mall culture, have all my insecurities solved through a "proper consumption" neither I nor my parents could readily afford.[40]

Loudermilk recognises the effect that *Dawn of the Dead* had on him in indulging his fantasies as a teenager struggling with consumer society's influence on mass and personal identity: "[P]art of the film's appeal when I first saw its trailer as a kid was the idea of four people having a mall all to themselves, and I remember prioritizing all I would do and possess… 'Mall Fantasia' sets in, for the characters and for me as spectator, and the film proves a thin line between fantasia and stupor."[41]

Loudermilk's experience certainly chimes with my own (we are of a similar age and background). Like Loudermilk, I was a proverbial small town boy who grew up in the late-1970s, into consumer-capitalist culture. However, my first exposure to *Dawn* was not at the movie theatre but at a 16mm screening, circa 1980, laid on at the social club of a large engineering company in the town that made road rollers, dump trucks and the like. The town, at that time, did not have a cinema, and so much of my movie-going was restricted to occasional 16mm screenings in social clubs and school halls. The first time I saw *Dawn of the Dead* was as a child of about thirteen; the screening was arranged for the children of the firm's workers, and was a mind-blowing experience. We teens couldn't believe what we were seeing because none of us had ever had access to such extreme material before (this was before home video became widely available). When the zombie took a bite out of the woman's arm early in the film, my friend turned to me said, "I think I'm going to be sick". The next month the same firm showed Romero's *Martin* (billed by word of mouth as "Martin the Vampire") because the *Dawn of the Dead* screening had been such a success. It felt like we were seeing things that were normally forbidden to us. That experience of watching *Dawn* in a hall on a 16mm projector as part of an audience of overexcited, overstimulated teenagers stayed with me. When VCRs came in, one of the first films I sought out was *Dawn of the Dead*, and, like many young fans, I could only dream of owning the film at a time when cassettes of new movies cost upwards of £25.

Dawn as a commodity (or "anti-commodity") to be consumed by fans, of course, plays into the very notion of fandom, and invokes a certain irony in relation to this film. Every fan of the *Dawn*, to an extent, feels that he or she somehow "owns" the film – and wants more of it. The ideological standpoint of "the more I consume, the more I demand to consume" applies well to *Dawn* and its fans. This is true of many cult films, but particularly so with *Dawn*. Re-releases on Blu-ray/ Ultra HD of *Dawn* by companies like Arrow and Second Sight are met with a feeding frenzy by fans who want more extras, more versions, more upgrades. Very few films feed so fervently into the fan's desire to "collect". Added to this is the popularity of the annual conventions surrounding *Dawn*. The largest of these is the *Living Dead Weekend* which takes place each year in the Monroeville Mall and in Evans City, outside of Pittsburgh. Here fans are able to buy merchandise, and, for a fee, collect autographs and have "photo opportunities" with many of the cast and crew of the movie. This is the fans' commodified "mecca": as the *Living Dead Weekend* website promises, "certain activities will take place after hours when the mall is typically closed to recreate that feeling of living in the set of the film", allowing fans to experience the "mall' fantasy (or at least aspects of it) for themselves.

The extent of *Dawn*'s fandom, however, goes beyond the comfortable consumption of the film, into areas of fan-based production. A number of fan-produced websites function as on-line resources for the film. Many of these, such as *WGON*, *Homepage of the Dead* and *The Zombie Farm*, are long-running concerns, and house a wealth of information about the film's production background, with on-set photographs, interviews with cast and crew, location shots and written analysis of the various different versions of the film. There are forums on which fans can interact and discuss every aspect of the film. Through web-related links, the fan is able to scrutinise the minutiae of *Dawn*: from its soundtrack, to its merchandise, its numerous video and DVD releases, posters and lobby cards, fan fiction and assorted memorabilia.

In terms of *Dawn*'s excess, it is clear that fans only want *more*. This is perhaps most apparent in the phenomenon of the fan-edit: new versions of the film assembled by fans using footage from the various different "official" cuts distributed internationally. Whilst fan-edits exist of other films (most notably a reconstruction from surviving frames of Tod Browning's 1927 lost film *London After Midnight* and a restructuring of Universal's *Murders in the Rue Morgue* [1932] to reflect the original intentions of its director Robert Florey), the various fan-edits of *Dawn* have one aim only: to reconstitute Romero's film in the longest form possible.

The first fan-edit of *Dawn* has been called "The Extended Mall Hours Cut". Assembled by a fan using footage from Romero's 139-minute Cannes Cut and Argento's 117-minute version, this was available as a bootleg DVD in the US. This fan-edit runs at 155 minutes and is thought to be the closest approximation to Romero's original assembly of the film. For years, fans demanded an official release of this version of the film. In 2018 German distributor XT Video released a 156-minute "Complete Cut" using the same footage, in response to fans who "wanted a cut of the film which contained all known mall footage and deleted scenes with nothing missing".[42] (Prior to that the longest "official" cut of the film has been the German-language 155-minute "Ultimate Final Cut", distributed by Astro Video.) Despite the fact that no new source material has since been found, there have been attempts by fans at longer cuts. Charles F. Gray has recently attempted a 161-minute 54-second version that would be

> the longest composite edit anyone could make, and that was using the three versions plus a couple of shots from the German trailer and some additional footage from the *Document Of The Dead* documentary neither of which are in any of the three versions. There have been two other composite edits produced and I know that my version would have been longer than both. The German language Astro "Ultimate Final Cut" DVD from 2001 running at 154m 38s (PAL or 161m 14s NTSC equivalent) which is about 40 seconds shorter, and the fanmade 'Extended Mall Hours Cut' DVD released in January 2008, edited by OfficiallyUnofficial running at 154m 35s (24P NTSC), which is about 7½ minutes shorter.[43]

As one DVD reviewer and *Dawn* fan puts it, "sometimes less is more, but with *Dawn of the Dead* you want all of it".[44]

FOOTNOTES

1. Tom Allen, "Knight of the Living Dead", *The Village Voice*, April 23, 1979, 1.

2. Quoted in http://broonsbane.tripod.com/dawndist.htm

3. George Anderson, "'Dawn of the Dead' – A Movie En-'grossing' in Every Way", *The Pittsburgh Post-Gazette*, May 8, 1979, 17.

4. "Dawn of the Dead", *Rotten Tomatoes*, https://www.rottentomatoes.com/m/1005339-dawn_of_the_dead

5. Ed Blank, "Locally Produced 'Dawn of the Dead' brings New Life to Horror", *The Pittsburgh Press*, April 13, 1979, 16.

6. Ibid.

7. Jones, "George Romero", *Starburst*, 38.

8. Quoted in Steven Swires, "George A. Romero: Master of the Living Dead", *Starlog* 21 (April, 1979), 47.

9. Lippe, Williams, and Wood, "The George Romero Interview, Toronto Film Festival, September 15th, 1979". *Cinema Spectrum*, 66.

10. "Blood and Gore Film", *The Pittsburgh Press*, April 24, 1979, 14.

11. Roger Ebert, "The Night of the Living Dead", *rogerebert.com*, January 5, 1969, https://www.rogerebert.com/reviews/the-night-of-the-living-dead-1968

12. "Letter", *The Pittsburgh Press*, April 20, 1979, 41.

13. Donald Miller, "'Dawn of the Dead' – Too long, Simple, Boring", *The Pittsburgh Post-Gazette*, April 14, 1979, 26.

14. Gary Arnold, "'Dawn of the Dead': Overdone Depravity", *The Washington Post*, May 4, 1979, 46.

15. *The Pittsburgh Post-Gazette*, April 24, 1979, 24.

16. Janet Maslin, "'Dawn of the Dead': Morning After", *New York Times*, April 20, 1979, 14.

17. Aaron Aradillas, "She's something else: Janet Maslin in a *rockcritics.com* interview", rockcritics.com, http://rockcriticsarchives.com/interviews/janetmaslin/janetmaslin.html

18. Quoted in Koetting, "No More Room in Hell", *The Dark Side*, 22.

19. Vincent Canby, "Getting Beyond Myra and The Valley of the Junk", *New York Times*, July 5, 1970, 49.

20. Wood, *Hollywood from Vietnam to Reagan*, 110

21. Pauline Kael, "Movies Opening", *The New Yorker*, April 18, 1979, 91.

22. Pauline Kael, *Hooked: Film Writings 1985 -1988* (London: Boyars, 1990), 67.

23. Ebert, "The Night of the Living Dead".

24. Roger Ebert, "'Dawn of the Dead': Sick or Subtle?", *The Pittsburgh Press*, May 6, 1979, 113.

25. Quoted in Ibid.

26. Lippe, Williams, and Wood, "The George Romero Interview, Toronto Film Festival, September 15th, 1979". *Cinema Spectrum*, 66-67.

27. Ibid.

28. Sharrett *Apocalypticism in the Contemporary Horror Film*, 237-238.

29. Ibid., 238.

30. Ibid., 251.

31. Christopher Sharrett, "The Horror Film as Social Allegory (And How it Comes Undone)" in Harry M. Benshoff, ed., *A Companion to the Horror Film*, (London: John Wiley & Sons, 2014), 63.

32. Ibid.

33. Ibid.

34. Ibid., 62-63.

35. Roger Ebert. "Last House on the Left", *rogerebert.com*, January 1, 1972, https://www.rogerebert.com/reviews/last-house-on-the-left-1972

36. Howard Thompson. "Last House on Left", *New York Times*, December 22, 1972, 21.

37. Linda Gross. "'Texas Massacre' Grovels in Gore", *Los Angeles Times*, October 30, 1974, 14.

38. Anderson, "'Dawn of the Dead' – A Movie En-'grossing' in Every Way", 20.

39. *The Pittsburgh Post-Gazette*, April 24, 1979, 24.

40. Loudermilk. "Eating 'Dawn' in the Dark: Zombie desire and commodified identity in George A. Romero's 'Dawn of the Dead'", 90.

41. Ibid., 93.

42. "Dawn of The Dead (1978) – 'Complete Cut' (XT Video) – Analysis & Review", *Neonfrights*, https://neonfrights.wordpress.com/2018/05/01/dawn-of-the-dead-1978-complete-cut-xt-video-analysis-review/

43. See https://www.facebook.com/groups/officialnightofthelivingdead/permalink/1673732526108518

44. "Dawn of The Dead (1978) – 'Complete Cut' (XT Video) – Analysis & Review", *Neonfrights*.

CHAPTER 6: "DEADENED BY BLOOD AND GORE": CENSORSHIP

Steffen Hantke has stated that capitalism "contains within itself contradictions, schisms, ruptures".[1] Historically, cinema can represent such a contradiction, schism, rupture. Sensational screen content arises from an economic imperative: to draw audiences into movie houses by ramping up the sex and violence. But such content can also pose moral and ideological threat, a schism between economic base and ideological superstructure which ultimately necessitates the introduction of tighter industry regulation and censorship in order to bring base and superstructure back into alignment. Although the excess of *Dawn of the Dead* polarized critics and shocked audiences, the biggest challenge it posed was to the film industry's censorship bodies. If *Dawn*'s excesses were part of the "economy of variation rather than rupture", as Barbara Klinger characterizes so-called "rebel texts", then this is only after censorship sought to bring the film into ideological alignment following disruption.

Dawn's financial success as an unrated film undermined the MPAA rating system, putting pressure on the MPAA to make changes to the system, pressure which the censorship body resisted for a number of years but which eventually resulted in the replacement of the "X"-rating with the "NC-17". In Britain – according to then BBFC president James Ferman – *Dawn* was considered a threat in terms of confronting the BBFC with "violence never before passed by the Board".[2] In Ontario, Canada it suffered severe cuts; and in Australia it was initially banned. Even in Germany and Japan (where it was released in the version prepared by Dario Argento) it was cut (extensively so in Japan).

Part of the threat *Dawn* posed to these censorship bodies arose undoubtedly because of its status as an independent film. Arguably, tougher standards were, and continue to be, imposed on independent distributors than on the Hollywood studios. *The Exorcist* is a case in point. Produced and distributed by Warner Brothers, it was released uncut in both the United States (where it was controversially rated only "R") and in the UK. Only six months after *Dawn* was released in the UK (in a heavily censored re-edited version by the BBFC), *Friday the 13th* (1980), which featured graphic violence comparable to that of *Dawn* (with special effects also by Tom Savini), was granted a BBFC certificate fully uncut. Like *The Exorcist*, *Friday the 13th* had the muscle of Warner Brothers behind it, something *Dawn* lacked. It might be argued that these studio films were felt by the censorship bodies to be mitigated by their essentially conservative moral messages; Romero's satire of consumer-capitalism was, by contrast, ideologically troubling to censors.

Another thorn in the censor's side, from the MPAA's perspective, was that Romero started a campaign against the "X" certificate being given to non-pornographic films; this he pursued in interviews and in an address to the National Association of Theatre Owners in Scottsdale, Arizona in April 1979, calling for a new, adults-only rating for films devoid of sexual content. This issue might have gone away if *Dawn* had not been such a box office success, prompting other distributors to release their films unrated, further undermining the American ratings system. Thus, when *Dawn* arrived at the BBFC it carried with it a certain amount of political controversy, and a wary James Ferman subjected *Dawn* to months of filibustering before finally granting it a release in a re-edited and watered-down version that Ferman himself oversaw. Indeed, it would be 24 years until the BBFC finally allowed *Dawn* to be seen in the UK in the uncut version that been on release in the States since 1979.

DAWN OF THE DEAD AND THE MPAA

Romero's objections to the prospect of the MPAA's Classification and Rating Administration (CARA) awarding *Dawn of the Dead* an "X" were twofold. Firstly, the punitive restrictions placed on "X"-rated films by prime-time television advertisers and newspapers (who refused to carry advertising for an "X"-rated film) would have a negative impact on the film's chances of success. Second, the "X" rating, in Gagne's words, had, by 1979, become "a symbol for sleaze in the minds of the American public".[3] In the rating system's early years, "X"-rated films such as *Midnight Cowboy* (1969) and *A Clockwork Orange* were understood to be unsuitable for children, but non-pornographic and intended for the general adult public. However, pornographic films often self-applied the non-trademarked "X" rating, and it soon became synonymous with pornography in American culture.

It is likely that Richard Heffner, who took over as president of the CARA board in 1974, sought to make an example of *Dawn* by burdening it with an "X" rating following the controversy of *The Exorcist* (during which the MPAA had faced considerable criticism for rating the film as acceptable for children to see). According to Jason Zinoman, after Heffner took over, he would spearhead efforts to be more aggressive with the "X" rating, especially over violence in films.[4] In 1976, Heffner had the board give the Japanese martial arts film *Gekitotsu! Satsujin ken* (*The Street Fighter*, 1974) an "X" rating for its graphic violence, the first time a film had earned that rating purely for violence. As previously mentioned, Heffner took it upon himself to phone Rubinstein personally to inform the producer that "there isn't a list of cuts long enough" for *Dawn* to avoid an "X": a clear indication of Heffner's intention to force the "X" certificate on Romero. However, Heffner had not bargained on the response of the independents. In a way, Heffner had backed Romero and Rubinstein into a corner, forcing them to release the film unrated in order to avoid the stigma of an "X". But Romero and Rubinstein were prepared to enter into what Gagne describes as "one of the independent film industry's most widely publicized, successful challenges to the American system"[5] and were vocal in interviews about their dismay at being pressured into an "X".

"We have no objection to the rating system," Rubinstein told the *Pittsburgh Post-Gazette* in February 1979, "but there is no category for adult entertainment that does not involve sex. The film will be released as George wants it, and we will be self-policing in order to limit the film to people 17 or older. But we want to avoid the X rating."[6] Rubinstein explained his reasons for wanting to avoid the "X" in an interview with *Variety*: "[S]ince there is no classification for an adult feature that happens not to have sexual content, we didn't want the misconception – or the economic sanctions – of an X rating."[7]

Rubinstein was at pains to emphasise that he and Romero were generally supportive of the American rating system, but was also candid about the double-standard at play in labelling a film like *Dawn* (which contains no sexual violence) as pornographic or obscene. Romero outlined his objections in an interview with the *Pittsburgh Post-Gazette*'s entertainment editor, George Anderson, which took place the following month in March, 1979. "My objection is not to the ratings system itself," he explained, "but to the fact that there is no category for adult entertainment that is devoid of sex… the MPAA needs a new ratings category because the X has become synonymous in the public mind with pornography… There is not a bit of sex or nudity in the film, but it is brutal. There's not a single scene, however, that hasn't been seen in some other film before. And all the violence is fantasy or comic book violence, like the old *Tales from the Crypt*."[8]

Heffner would probably not have been worried when Laurel and UFD decided to take the route of distributing *Dawn* unrated, no doubt assuming that the film would become marginalized as a result. Its subsequent box office success, however, proved an irritant to the MPAA, especially when some exhibitors failed to adhere to the self-imposed age restriction and promoted the film as an "R"-rated picture, undermining the system further. This prompted Jack Valenti (the head of the MPAA) himself to issue a press statement addressing the issue in no uncertain terms:

> Some theaters that are playing *Dawn of the Dead* designate at the box office that the film has been rated R. This is not true. They are using the R in an unwarranted fashion, as this film has not been rated at all, and we will commence legal action against anyone who persists in misusing the R. The G, PG, and R symbols are registered with the U.S Patent Office as certification marks of the Motion Picture Association of America Inc. and their unauthorized use in any way will be subject to legal action.[9]

Despite the threat of legal action, a number of cinemas continued to advertise *Dawn* as an "R"-rated film during its initial release. As if this wasn't enough to draw attention to the deficiencies of CARA, by July 1979, the film's box office bonanza was already prompting industry commentators (such as Tom Allen at the *Village Voice*) to predict a change to "the way films are made, rated and marketed in America".[10] Suddenly the whole rating system was open to question. "The policy review committee of the Code and Ratings Administration has been discussing proposed changes in the movie ratings system, especially concerning the X," reported the *Pittsburgh Post-Gazette* on July 3, 1979. "George Romero recently proposed an adults-only category for films like his *Dawn of the Dead* that have no sex content. Jack Valenti opposes the idea."[11]

Valenti would, in fact, continue to oppose the idea until 1990 when – facing renewed criticism for the lack of a designation for adult films like *Henry Portrait of a Serial Killer* (1989) and *The Cook, The Thief, His Wife and Her Lover* (1989) – the MPAA finally replaced the "X"-rating with the "NC-17". However, media pressure on the MPAA had already started to grow in 1979 with *Dawn*'s success and the attention given to Romero by the national press – with interviews in the *New York Times*, *Variety* and a front-page profile in the *Village Voice* which dubbed him the "Knight of the Living Dead" for the challenges that *Dawn* posed to the American system. Other filmmakers and distributors saw the success of *Dawn* as an unrated feature and took note. By September 1980, a flood of unrated films hit the American market, prompting industry commentators to predict the death of the "X"-rating. "The X rating may be vanishing except as an unintended lure for porno theatres," wrote the *Pittsburgh Post-Gazette*. "The commercial success of films as diverse as *Dawn of the Dead* and *Caligula* (1979) – which were released with no rating because their distributors refused to accept an X – may have tolled the death knell for the X." Among the films released unrated would include Lucio Fulci's *Zombi* (1979), Troma's *Mother's Day*, and Nicolas Roeg's *Bad Timing* (1980). The latter was considered particularly significant as a "serious" film from the director of *Don't Look Now* (1973) and *The Man Who Fell to Earth* (1976) and had also won first prize at that year's Toronto Film Festival. "When the ratings system started 10 years ago," the *Pittsburgh Post-Gazette* concluded, "most theaters refused to play unrated films, but that is no longer true. Anything that does business will be booked."[12]

JAPAN, WEST GERMANY, ONTARIO AND AUSTRALIA

By the time the Argento cut of *Dawn* had been submitted to Japan's national censor in early 1980, the film had already been rejected by the MPAA and censorship bodies in Australia and the United Kingdom. The resulting censorship of *Dawn* in Japan took on a distinctly bizarre form. The Herald Enterprises print, which opened in six cinemas in Tokyo and Osaka on March 13, 1979, freezes frames before each gore sequence, and then resumes motion after the offending footage is over, in effect announcing to the viewer the fact that scenes have been censored. The use of optical printing had become commonplace in film censorship in Japan, with shots reframed or blurred to obscure offending footage, especially during sex scenes; one can only assume that a Japanese audience had grown used to the visual distraction of material censored in this way. More disturbing to a Japanese audience, it seems, would have been Romero's lack of an explanation for the zombie outbreak; Nippon Herald Films added its own pre-title sequence at the start of the film which gave the reason for the phenomenon as radiation "from an exploding planet in a far off galaxy" which "caused the transformation of the dead one after another into resurrected zombies seeking the flesh of the living". This addition to Argento's cut does recast the film as a more conventional science fiction entry in the tradition of Japanese-American co-productions such as *Ganma Daisan Gō: Uchū Daisakusen* (*The Green Slime*, 1968), making *Dawn* more palatable to local audiences.

Changes made by Neue Constantin Film and the West German censor were less sweeping. With only a few cuts made to Argento's version, *Dawn* opened in 60 West German cinemas on August 3, 1979, with key venues in Berlin, Dusseldorf, Frankfurt, Munich, Stuttgart and a number of other cities. The distributor poured money into the release, and Romero himself went on a publicity tour of West Germany and Austria in the summer of 1979. Neue Constantin Film's investment paid off, as did Japan's. In November that year *Variety* reported *Dawn*'s grosses in those countries as "hefty": $3million in Japan and $5.2 million in Germany.[13] In West Germany, *Dawn* did bigger box office than had *The Exorcist*, attracting an audience of three million. In *Danse Macabre*, Stephen King speculates on the reasons for its popularity in Germany, where, in his words, "*Dawn of the Dead* went through the roof". He writes:

> *The Exorcist* (a social horror film if ever there was one) did only so-so business when it was released in West Germany, a country which had an entirely different set of social fears at the time (they were a lot more worried about bomb-throwing radicals than about foul-talking young people).[14]

This may, in fact, account for some of *Dawn*'s attraction to its young West German audience, many of whom, at the time of the Red Army Faction, would have been in sympathy with the anti-consumerist message on screen and the violence perpetrated against the symbols of consumer-capitalism. This element of the film's social context may have, in fact, influenced other censorship boards in Europe who detected in *Dawn* a tacit approval of the violent actions of terrorist organisations like the Baader-Meinhoff Group. Certainly the biker gang sequence at the end of the film seems to key into the mythologising of left-wing militant groups of the time as modern day outlaws or bandits.

Fears of encouraging looting and other anti-social and criminal behaviour may well have influenced Ontario's initial decision to ban *Dawn of the Dead*. As Richard Rubinstein revealed at the Toronto Film Festival in September 1979, "At first the Ontario censor refused it totally so we had to tell them, 'It's not meant to be taken seriously.' They said, 'Oh?' It's so highly stylized and exaggerated as to be absurd black comedy."[15] Even so, the Ontario board made drastic cuts to *Dawn* when it was released there in the autumn of 1980, taking out 13 minutes. "We are a cause célèbre in Ontario,"[16] Romero told *Starburst* in 1982, decrying the lack of logic and motivation in the board's decision to render the film virtually incomprehensible through censorship cuts. Audiences openly booed the censor in the cinema and wrote to the newspapers complaining about the notoriously scissor-happy Ontario Film Review Board. Indeed, Ontario filmgoers had grown increasingly frustrated with the censor's heavy-handed treatment of adult-themed releases, which resulted in a series of high-profile disputes with the Toronto Film Festival when a number of critically acclaimed international titles such as Louis Malle's *Pretty Baby* (1978) and Volker Schlöndorff's *The Tin Drum* (1980) were refused screenings without cuts, or banned outright.

Excessive violence was the reason why *Dawn* was refused registration by the Australian Classification Board in November 1978, where it was first submitted in Dario Argento's cut. It would be submitted a total of four times before finally being granted an "R" in a heavily censored form. In fact, *Dawn*'s censorship history in Australia closely mirrors that of Britain. The question has to be raised why Argento's non-English language version was submitted in the first place – Argento's deal with Laurel was for non-English speaking world rights. The film was submitted to the board by Sydney-based subsidiary Incamera Pty Ltd., but after it was refused a certificate, *Dawn*'s distribution in Australia remained in limbo for fifteen months. In October, 1979 United Artists (who now owned the Australian rights) submitted Romero's American theatrical cut, but that too was banned due to "excessive violence". Following an unsuccessful appeal to the Films Board of Review in November, 1979, UA resubmitted *Dawn* in a "reconstructed soft version" that was a minute shorter than the previously submitted Romero cut. That too was rejected for "excessive violence". UA submitted the film for the third time in February 1980 with further cuts totalling 40 seconds. Who actually made these cuts for UA – whether it was Romero himself or an in-house editor – remains unclear. UA made an additional 23 seconds of cuts before the Classification Board awarded the "R" for "Restricted

Exhibition" reserved for films with frequent and high levels of violence. By the time of its release on April 3, 1980, *Dawn* had lost over two minutes from Romero's theatrical cut.[17] Yet this was still less than would be taken out by the British censor when *Dawn* was finally released in the UK as *Zombies: Dawn of the Dead* on June 29, 1980.

DAWN OF THE DEAD AND THE BBFC.

Although *Dawn* was extensively cut by Ontario and Australia, it would be the (then titled) British Board of Film Censors that would take the greatest offence to Romero's film and its message. No doubt influenced by the problems encountered by the MPAA when UFD decided to go unrated, the chief British censor would seek to recut *Dawn* himself in a bid to render what he described as a "desensitising and disgusting wallow in the ghoulish details of violence"[18] into something more acceptable for an "X" certificate. Although personally overseeing the re-cutting of films was apparently not unheard of for James Ferman, it is somewhat at odds with practice elsewhere. The Australian Classification Board, for example, did not dictate cuts or order changes to the film, but instead left it to United Artists to make cuts. The ACB exercised censorship by refusing classification, by simply saying "yes" or "no" to proposed changes by the distributor, which is why United Artists had to re-edit and re-submit *Dawn* three times in all. Perhaps Ferman's idiosyncratic handling of *Dawn* explains why Rubinstein, Romero and the BBFC all give conflicting accounts of the film's censorship in the UK.

According to Rubinstein, Ferman had originally wanted to take ten minutes out of *Dawn* when Argento's version was originally submitted for classification in June 1979. "The distributor was very upset about this," Rubinstein told Paul R. Gagne in 1987. "Furman [sic] wanted to cut out all the 'goodies'. We then showed him *our* version… He only wanted to take thirty seconds out of our version, and he explained himself – 'I now understand: there *is* a rationale for this violence'."[19] Romero, however, told *Starburst* in 1982 that "there are less than three minutes cut altogether".[20] Where Romero and Rubinstein do concur is in their claim that it was Argento's version of *Dawn* that caused the problems at the BBFC rather than Ferman's filibustering. As Romero explained to *Starburst*:

When the film was first presented to the censor here it was the Dario's European version which was felt to be very exploitative with the result that a lot was cut. The distributor (Target International Pictures) freaked out over that version and decided to submit the American version instead. The censor then felt that the film was softened so much by the values that the humour injected that they decided to leave a lot in that they had cut from the previous version. I had a dialogue with censor Jim Ferman which is something that I have never had anywhere else in the world. Logic and motivation was applied which is the direct opposite of what happened in Ontario.[21]

The BBFC's own account makes no reference to the Argento version at all (again, the question must be asked why the distributor would submit the non-English language version for the British market). What they do admit is that the film arrived in June 1979 with a certain amount of "notoriety" in terms of its unrated release in the US and Romero's clashes with the MPAA. This may have biased the six examiners and James Ferman against the film from the start. The BBFC records show that the six examiners disliked the film, and all agreed, together with Ferman, that it would need to be cut before release to the general public. Ferman stated that the film featured violence "to a degree never before passed by the Board", and demanded 55 cuts amounting to two minutes and 17 seconds of screen time. Target made these cuts and resubmitted the film in July. However, despite Target meeting the Board's demands, Ferman re-examined the film with a new team of examiners, all of whom disliked the film (some of whom felt that a certificate should not be granted at all due to the potentially damaging effect of the film's violent scenes on the viewer). Ferman ordered further cuts (exactly how many is not clear). Target made these and submitted the film for a third time. Ferman then re-examined the film himself and asked Target to cut *another* one minute and 29 seconds from the running time.

By this point, Target began to worry that *Dawn* would not be ready for its screening at the London Film Festival in November.[22] Ferman, of course, knew then that he held the distributor over a barrel. He suggested that his "in-house editor" make a cut of the film that would be acceptable for an "X" certificate (this despite the numerous cuts that the BBFC had already asked Target to make over the previous months). Who this "in-house editor" was remains unknown;[23] however, it is almost certainly the case that Ferman would have supervised the editing personally. In September, 1979, Ferman sent a letter to Target informing them:

> a tour de force of virtuoso editing has transformed this potential reject from a disgusting and desensitising wallow in the ghoulish details of violence and horror to a strong, but more conventional action piece… The cutting is not only skilful, but creative, and I think it has actually improved a number of the sequences by making the audience notice the emotions of the characters and the horror of the situation instead of being deadened by blood and gore.[24]

Romero and Rubinstein were clearly very diplomatic in interviews when it came to discussing *Dawn*'s treatment by the BBFC. Certainly, they would have been aware of the politics involved, given the "notoriety" of the film and its censorship controversy in the States and elsewhere. Perhaps they were simply relieved that Ferman had – at least – not rendered the film incomprehensible by censor cuts as it had been in Ontario. The UK market was a lucrative one, and Laurel needed the distribution deal. Romero told *Starburst* in 1982, "on an absolute level, of course we would prefer not to have the film touched at all. This is the real world, however, and I don't think people will get any less enjoyment from it as it now stands… as far as I'm concerned the intention or texture of the film hasn't been affected at all".[25]

But there is a sense in which that is not true. The argument put forward by the BBFC supporting their censoring of *Dawn* was based on the concern that the film's excessive violence would have a possible desensitising effect on vulnerable audiences, hence Ferman's comment in his letter to Target about the audience being "deadened by blood and gore". This argument is, of course, an old one within film censorship, and open to debate. As David Trend comments in his book *The Myth of Media Violence*, "This line of reasoning leads some in the media violence field to believe that repeated exposure to extreme depictions of brutality desensitizes audiences to violent representations and makes them less concerned about violence in real life. Others contend that audiences of 'splatter' classics like *Re-animator* (1985) and *Brain Damage* (1987)…see the movies as funny because of their outrageous excesses of gore which reveals the movie's ironic intent."[26] It is clear from the BBFC records that the examiners of *Dawn of the Dead* took the former, rather than the latter view. As the BBFC records state:

Much discussion was given over to the moral framework of the film – were the zombies sentient beings or unfeeling objects; was the violence mitigated by the fact that the zombies are no longer human beings; was the audience being invited to indulge in the killings because the zombies ostensibly felt nothing?[27]

The BBFC also relates that one of the examiners apparently felt so strongly that the film glorifies violence that "he excluded himself from any further screenings or discussions surrounding the work".[28] This hardly inspires confidence in the BBFC's ability to conduct a rational debate about the issue of desensitisation in films, at least in the case of *Dawn of the Dead*. Certainly, Romero's intention – as stated explicitly by him on a number of occasions – was at odds with BBFC examiners' reading of the film. The BBFC's view was also at odds with the readings of a number of film reviewers. In one of the earliest write-ups, by Ed Blank of the *Pittsburgh Press* (April 13, 1979) it is commented that the film is "filled with revolting sights, yet it isn't a nightmare. It can't be. At least one of the leading men behaves anti-heroically – taking astonishing pleasure in pulverising and blowing apart the zombies. The effect on an even slightly sensitive audience is distancing."[29] This was precisely Romero's aim – to create a kind of Brechtian *Verfremdungseffekt*. As Tom Savini recalled in the documentary *The American Nightmare*, "George's intention, if I'm quoting him correctly, was to numb you to the violence. Which is what happened to me in Vietnam. You get numb after a while. After you've seen so many bodies, it's just like another thing."[30] Romero himself clarifies this in the documentary: "[Y]ou're meant to be uncomfortable there. And that puts you in a kind of a mindset to accept the other ideas in the film, I think. It opens your mind a little more to those ideas."[31]

Clearly, numbing the audience with shock to make them uncomfortable with on-screen violence is very different to desensitising the viewer in such a way as they become inured to violence in real life. Why, then, did Ferman persist in describing the film as "a disgusting and desensitising wallow in the ghoulish details of violence" without consideration of Romero's intentions, even after the dialogue that Romero claims to have taken place between them (during which Romero would surely have made his intentions clear to the censor)? Could it be that it was to "the other ideas in the film" that Ferman and his examiners *really* objected?[32]

Interestingly, one of the most censored sequences in *Dawn of the Dead* is the shopping mall massacre, where Fran, Stephen, Roger and Peter slaughter the zombies in order to claim the mall as their own. Prior to that we have seen Stephen and Peter raid the mall's gun store in order to arm themselves; the tribal music that Romero plays over this scene emphasises the frontiership theme that comes to the fore in this section of the film. In the script Romero comments, "we recognize the firepower in the arsenal that the two men accumulate".[33] Indeed, that firepower is such that the massacre of the zombies takes on a deeply ambivalent inflection when seen in the uncensored versions, bringing home the brutality of the slaughter. Instead of feeling exhilarated as the group claims the mall from the zombies, we begin to feel a sense of moral disgust at the scale of the zombie massacre. "We see the men wheeling garden carts piled with corpses," Romero writes in the script. "The somber image is shocking as the figures move in silhouette against the bright store fronts with their displays of goods designed to attract shoppers to the sweet life the items pretend to represent."[34] Ferman's cut of the film, by contrast, diminishes the sense of revulsion at the zombie massacre, instead turning the sequence into a "more conventional action piece".

Of course, the self-congratulatory tone of Ferman's letter to Target suggests that he really did see himself as the hero of the hour. Possibly he was concerned that the film's violence would set a precedent (certainly, the BBFC would take a firm stand against the slasher cycle that was shortly to come into being following the box office success of *Friday the 13th*). He also knew that *Dawn of the Dead*, because of its history at the MPAA, was a problematic film politically. Perhaps he genuinely did see the film as exploitative and desensitising, despite Romero's intentions with it. Maybe he felt he had done Romero a favour with his "tour de force of virtuoso editing" that, in his eyes, improved the film. Finally, perhaps, Ferman was just trying to please everyone involved by finding a way out of the problem.

However, that does not account for the fact that *Dawn of the Dead* would have to wait another 24 years until the BBFC would allow it go out uncut on VHS and DVD, while, in the meantime, a number of other "splatter" classics would be passed without cuts by BBFC examiners. Peter Jackson's *Braindead* (1992) is a case in point. In the UK, *Braindead* was shown in its full 104-minute uncut version with an "18" certificate, and the British Board of Film Classification even considered lowering the certificate to a

"15", because the censors thought that the film was hilarious. "I don't much care for horror spoofs," wrote one BBFC reviewer in his report, "but this is wonderfully funny – a genuinely entertaining Grand Guignol farce in which the pace never flags… I was strongly tempted to go for '15' despite the endless succession of amputated limbs, torn-off head-skins, beheadings, buckets of blood, dismemberments, pustules bursting, arms being devoured; on and on the comic gore is piled but not without genuine comic structure so that each sight of entire rib cages being torn out, heads being whipped up in a blender and so on is continuously varied by a truly original comic sense."

The censor goes on to discuss how much he and his colleagues enjoyed the film's sickest scene involving the liquidising of a zombie baby. "The attempt to stuff a wonderfully vicious zombie baby into the blender results in a series of sight gags which had us all in hysterics. In fact, I don't think I've laughed so much at a film all year." "In the end I went along with '18' simply on the pragmatic grounds that most people would expect the astonishing amount of gore here to be '18'," the BBFC reviewer concludes, "[b]ut I can't imagine even a sensitive teenager being bothered by this." Other BBFC examiners were just as gushing in their praise of *Braindead*, describing how the film's OTT farce and clever editing had the whole team "rolling about in mirth". "There's none of that undercurrent of cruelty and personalised violence that concerned us in *The Evil Dead* films or *Demons 2*. *Braindead* is played for belly laughs rather than screams or ghoulish chuckles, and it's much less heartless than the recent *Rabid Grannies* (passed '18' uncut)."[35] *Dawn of the Dead*, by contrast, with its equally excessive Grand Guignol, but with a tacit observation of alternative ideologies and countercultural values, would not be released uncut in the UK until twelve years after *Braindead*.

Despite the liberalisation of film classification boards generally since *Dawn*'s release, the film has continued to be censored in such countries as Germany (where all DVD and Blu-ray releases have been censored), suggesting that its extremity has posed a genuine ideological threat. What censors seem to have objected to is not just the excessive violence but the savage irony with which the violence was deployed by Romero. *Dawn of the Dead* succeeds in making us uncomfortable with the underlying assumptions that form the bedrock of our culture.

FOOTNOTES

1. Steffen Hantke, "Capitalist Horrors", *Other Voices: The ejournal of Cultural Criticism*, Vol. 3, No.1 (May, 2007), accessed November 22, 2014, http://www.othervoices.org/3.1/shantke/index.php

2. Letter, James Ferman to Target International Pictures, September 7th, 1979, "Dawn of the Dead" file, *BBFC*.

3. Gagne, *The Zombies That Ate Pittsburgh: The Films of George A. Romero*, 98.

4. Jason Zinoman, *Shock Value* (New York: The Penguin Press, 2011), 109.

5. Gagne, *The Zombies That Ate Pittsburgh: The Films of George A. Romero*, 97.

6. George Anderson, "The Triangle Tattler", *The Pittsburgh Post-Gazette*, February 5, 1979, 16.

7. Quoted in Koetting, "No More Room in Hell", *The Dark Side*, 21.

8. George Anderson, "The Triangle Tattler", *The Pittsburgh Post-Gazette*, March 8, 1979, 18.

9. Source: Schöfböck, "History", *WGON*, http://www.dawnofthedead.co.uk/history/

10. Allen, "Knight of the Living Dead", *The Village Voice*, 1.

11. George Anderson, "The Triangle Tattler", *The Pittsburgh Post-Gazette*, July 3, 1979, 18.

12. "X-ed out", *The Pittsburgh Post-Gazette*, September 30, 1980, 21.

13. Quoted in "Festive Horror", *The Pittsburgh Post-Gazette*, November 21, 1979, 19.

14. Stephen King, *Danse Macabre*, (London: Futura Publications, 1982), 156.

15. Lippe, Williams, and Wood, "The George Romero Interview, Toronto Film Festival, September 15, 1979". *Cinema Spectrum*, 67.

16. Jones, "George Romero", *Starburst*, 36.

17. Source: https://www.classification.gov.au/

18. Letter, James Ferman to Target International Pictures, September 7, 1979.

19. Gagne, *The Zombies That Ate Pittsburgh: The Films of George A. Romero*, 97.

20. Jones, "George Romero", *Starburst*, 36.

21. Ibid.

22. Source: "Dawn of the Dead" file, *BBFC*.

23. Tim Murray confirms that the BBFC didn't have an in-house editor and that, according to his source at the BBFC, such cuts to films submitted for certification "usually would be done by a projectionist, under direction from a BBFC member of staff (normally James Ferman)". Murray, "Dawn of the Nasties", in *George A. Romero's Dawn of the Dead: Dissecting the Dead*, DVD extra, Second Sight Films, 2020.

24. Letter, James Ferman to Target International Pictures, September 7, 1979.

25. Jones, "George Romero", *Starburst*, 36.

26. David Trend, *The Myth of Media Violence: A Critical Introduction*, (Oxford: Blackwell Publishing, 2007), 90-91.

27. Source: Dawn of the Dead file, *BBFC*.

28. Ibid.

29. Blank, "Locally Produced 'Dawn of the Dead' brings New Life to Horror", *The Pittsburgh Press*, April 13, 1979, 16.

30. Adam Simon, *The American Nightmare*, IFC, 1999.

31. Ibid.

32. The BBFC's argument around the censoring of the film ties a specific brand of elitism, but also, I would suggest, a strain of post-WWII paternalism that is present in many aspects of UK life (urban planning, technocracy, etc.).

33. George A. Romero, *Dawn of the Dead*, Working Draft, 1977, 140.

34. Ibid., 160.

35. Source: "Braindead file", *BBFC*.

AFTERWORD: "ALIVE TO THE SOUND OF MUZAK"

Critical theorists and economists tell us that we have moved on from the era of consumer-capitalism. According to some we are now in the age of "disaster capitalism", a time in which governments profit from (inter)national crises by sending in private companies to deal with the problem. Disasters prop up the economy, and make politicians wealthy. Meanwhile, the authorities effectively turn their backs on the population, whilst Hollywood performs the cultural work necessary to preserve the hegemony.

Of course, not all sci-fi-horror-disaster movies seek to rehabilitate patriarchal authority. There are a few entries in the genre which depict authority as ultimately disclaiming responsibility for the welfare of those under its protection, but those films are in the minority. Perhaps the most influential in this regard has been *Night of the Living Dead*, whose zombie apocalypse brings about a collapse of society exacerbated by patriarchal institutions. In Romero's film, Washington officials are seen retreating from reporters seeking clarification, aid and information about the zombie virus on the public's behalf. When advice is given by the authorities on how to survive the attacks, it is confusing, sporadic and changes hourly. At first people are told to stay in their homes, and then later they are told to risk travelling to rescue centres for evacuation from the towns and cities.

The authorities in *Night of the Living Dead* have in effect abandoned the population and it is left to vigilante groups to enforce order. Meanwhile, would-be patriarchal heroes like Ben and Harry are too busy engaged in a pissing contest to lead the other survivors to safety. Each man's inability to defer to the other's plan of action (both of which are shown to be mistaken, incidentally) prevents the rest of the group from accepting the authority of either, leaving the voices of reason to the eldest woman (Harry's wife, Helen) and the youngest male, Tom, both of whom are ignored because of their place in the group hierarchy.

Romero expanded on these themes in *Dawn of the Dead*, in which we witness authority figures within law enforcement and the emergency services deserting their posts as the disaster strikes. Those who remain act irresponsibly towards the public, like the TV station manager who knowingly broadcasts erroneous civil defence information, risking the lives of many. Government figures are conspicuous by their absence (presumably all have flown off to their private islands), again leaving law and order in the hands of beer-swilling rednecks who seem to be rather enjoying the whole thing.

How could Romero have gotten it so right?

The extremity of *Dawn* continues to be enjoyed by audiences around the world. Its resonance is just as profound now, in the age of "disaster capitalism", as it was in the 1970s – if not more so. Now *Dawn* can be consumed on Ultra High Definition, fully uncut, in Germany, America, France, England and even Ontario. And soon – as promised by Richard Rubinstein himself – in glorious digital 3D, with its "splatter" comin' at ya.

Like its zombies, *Dawn* will not stay dead. It is, and continues to be – as the *Pittsburgh Press* quipped in 1979 – "alive to the sound of Muzak".[1]

FOOTNOTES

1.   Ebert, "'Dawn of the Dead': Sick or Subtle?", *The Pittsburgh Press*, May 6, 1979, 113.

DEVIL'S ADVOCATES

"Auteur Publishing's new Devil's Advocates critiques on individual titles offer bracingly fresh perspectives from passionate writers. The series will perfectly complement the BFI archive volumes." Christopher Fowler, Independent on Sunday

CREEPSHOW – SIMON BROWN

Simon Brown's analysis focuses on the key influences on the film, alongside those of George Romero and Stephen King – the anthology horrors of Amicus, body horror cinema, the special make-up effects of Tom Savini, and the tradition of EC horror comics of the 1950s.

THE OMEN – ADRIAN SCHOBER

Adrian Schober's Devil's Advocate covers the genesis, authorship, production history, marketing and reception of The Omen, before going on to examine the overarching theme of paranoia that drives the narrative.

THE TEXAS CHAIN SAW MASSACRE – JAMES ROSE

As well as providing a summary of the making of the film, James Rose discusses its extraordinary censorship history in the UK and provides a detailed textual analysis of the film with particular reference to the concept of 'the Uncanny'.